CHRISTOPHER CATHERWOOD is Emeritus Archives By-Fellow of Churchill College Cambridge, Fellow of the Royal Historical Society and a regular supervisor for Homerton College, Cambridge. He has written many books and articles including *Winston's Folly* and *A Brief History of the Middle East*.

By Christopher Catherwood

The Battles of WWI: Everything You Need to Know
The Battles of WWII: Everything You Need to Know

a&b

THE BATTLES OF WORLD WAR II:

Everything You Need to Know

CHRISTOPHER CATHERWOOD

Allison & Busby Limited
12 Fitzroy Mews
London W1T 6DW
www.allisonandbusby.com

First published in Great Britain by Allison & Busby in 2014.

A CIP catalogue record for this book is available from
the British Library.

First Edition

ISBN 978-0-7490-1507-7

Typeset in 10.75/15.75 pt Adobe Garamond Pro by
Allison & Busby Ltd.

The paper used for this Allison & Busby publication
has been produced from trees that have been legally sourced
from well-managed and credibly certified forests.

Printed and bound by
CPI Group (UK) Ltd, Croydon, CR0 4YY

To
Geoffrey Drinkwater
Fleet Air Arm and
Veteran of the Arctic Convoys

To
Alan Clough
Queen's Bays
Veteran of North Africa and Italy

and to my wife
Paulette
Niece of Lacy Foster Paulette Jr
Veteran of the Battle of the Bulge.

TABLES OF CONTENTS

INTRODUCTION

PART ONE

1937–1939

Prelude to War and Beginning Short

PART TWO: I

1939–1941

Early War: Western Europe

PART TWO: II

1941–1942

Early War: The Eastern Front

PART TWO: III

1941–1942

The USA Enters the War

PART THREE: I

1941–1942

The Eastern Front

PART FOUR: III

1942–1943

The War Against Japan

PART FIVE: I

1944–1945

The Western Allies in Europe

PART FIVE: II

1944

The Eastern Front

PART FIVE: III

1944

The War Against Japan

PART SIX: I

1945

The Eastern Front

PART SIX: II

1945

The Western Front and
the End of the War in Europe

PART SIX: III

1945

The War Against Japan and the End of the Fighting

INTRODUCTION

THE WAR OF THE MILLENNIUM

No conflict ever fought has been like World War II. The sheer carnage is staggering. Experts now reckon that over eighty million people died as a result of the war; this is without parallel in human history. Since an unusually large percentage of that number were civilians, ordinary folk living far from what they thought were the battlefields, the Second World War was more horrific than any conflict for centuries, since the Mongol invasions of the thirteenth century. In Europe no such death toll of innocent lives had occurred since the Thirty Years War over 300 years earlier. World War II, especially the fighting on the Eastern Front between the Germans and the USSR, is often called the 'War of the Century' but one can argue that 'War of the Millennium' might be a better title.

THE SCALE OF WAR: THE UNIQUENESS
OF DEATH AND DESTRUCTION

This book is about some of the key individual battles fought during this unique conflict. By definition, therefore, we will be looking mainly at military deaths. We will also consider the bombing raids, which entailed mainly civilian casualties, such as the Blitz in London, and the attacks on German and Japanese cities.

Even the battles themselves have deaths on a scale unimaginable before the war began – for example, over twelve million Red Army troops were killed in the fight against Germany in 1941–1945, a toll that dwarfs even the carnage of the First World War. But along with those deaths, it is now reckoned that some fifteen million civilians also died in those four years, a figure therefore higher than the slaughter in the battles that will be described in our book. All six million of the Jewish deaths in the Holocaust were also civilian and the same horrors would apply to most of the twenty million Chinese killed by the Japanese. War is normally about battles, but this struggle was different.

Before we go on to look at the battles, we need to consider the origins and causes of the Second World War. We also need to examine the question: when and where did the Second World War begin?

In my previous book *The Battles of World War I*, we asked at the start 'why were they enemies', 'what led to the war' and 'was war inevitable'? In some ways it is easier to answer these questions when studying World War II. No one doubts that Germany was unquestionably the aggressor this time. The Nazis, Italy and Japan were all guilty. So we know whom the main enemies were, and that the aggression of Germany and Japan led to war.

Italy fought against the Allies 1940–1943, joining the Third Reich in 1940 out of opportunism when it looked as if Hitler would win, and leaving it in 1943, when Benito Mussolini was overthrown. We will look at Italy in this book but what that country did was not as vital as Germany and Japan.

But while the aggressors are known and undisputed, much discussion has taken place over the 'what led to war' question, to which we now turn.

WHEN WHERE AND
WHY DID WAR BEGIN?

The Second World War is often thought of as the 'good war'. But that is because we think of it entirely in relation to the Western war: of the British plucky resistance to Adolf Hitler in 1940, of the Americans, Canadians and British on D-Day and afterwards in 1944, and for American readers, the gigantic scale battles between the USA and Japan in the Pacific.

But the story is in fact more complex than that.

British and Commonwealth countries mark the beginning of armed conflict as September 3rd 1939, with the German invasion of Poland. The Russians joined the war on June 22nd 1941 when Germany invaded their country. The bombing of Pearl Harbor on December 7th 1941 marked the beginning of hostilities for the USA. As President Franklin Roosevelt told the

American people when declaring war on Japan the following day, the 7th was 'a date which will live in infamy'.

However, a new school of thought dates the war as beginning on July 7th 1937, with World War II opening, not in Europe or Hawaii, but in Beijing. To this way of thinking, the Sino-Japanese war of 1937–1945 morphed into the wider conflict in 1941 and can thus be seen as the real start of the global conflict as a whole. One of our battles, therefore, will be the Japanese capture and massacre of Nanjing in 1937.

In this case the war was under way two years before Hitler started to invade various countries in 1939, and we need to rethink how we consider the war. We shall look in detail at the 'Marco Polo Bridge Incident' later on, when fighting broke out in 1937 between Chinese and Japanese troops near Beijing. Certainly we need to have it in mind as we look at the more familiar story of Hitler and the struggle for Europe.

And we should not forget that Britain, the Netherlands and France had large colonies in East Asia back then, not to mention the biggest of all, the British Raj in South Asia, all of which were threatened by Japan even if war against the British and Dutch colonies did not actually start until 1941. Thousands of Americans lived in China as missionaries, and the USA had a long history of active involvement in that region, not least because they ruled the Philippines. So while this chapter will be more Eurocentric, the desire of Japan to expand at the expense of China and of the European ruled parts of Asia is a very major factor in the war.

And let us not forget that in the First World War, Japan and Italy were allies of Britain, France and of their associated power, the USA.

Let us return now to Europe and to 1933.

THE ORIGINS OF WORLD WAR II IN EUROPE: A NEW PERSPECTIVE

No Hitler, no Second World War . . . This seems obvious, yet we forget that perhaps World War II was not as inevitable as we often consider it.

In the 1920s Germany actually recovered from the economic crisis that afflicted it in the immediate aftermath of 1918. We usually recall the riots and near-Communist revolution in Berlin, and Hitler's attempt to seize power in Munich. However, we forget that Germany recovered from its inner turmoil and settled down to being a fairly prosperous country ready to put its defeat behind it.

In 1925 the victorious countries of the Great War – the USA, United Kingdom and France – signed the Locarno Treaty in Switzerland with Germany. In essence Germany recognised its *Western* borders and in effect promised to behave. The Americans now gave Germany massive financial credits, which in turn created a virtuous circle, since this enabled Germany to pay (much reduced) reparation payments to France and Britain. This money in turn enabled the United Kingdom and France to repay their war debts to the USA. In 1925 the British Foreign Secretary Sir Austen Chamberlain (Neville's half-brother) was given the Nobel Prize for the Locarno Treaty, and the German Chancellor, Gustav Stresemann, received it in 1926 for similar contributions to peace between Germany and France.

The 'Locarno Honeymoon', the name given to the euphoria in Western Europe that peace would now be permanent, meant that everyone felt happy and safe. And Winston Churchill, as Chancellor of the Exchequer, kept going an earlier British policy, the Ten Year Rule. This measure drastically lowered British defence expenditure because politicians were certain there would be no war for at least ten years ahead. If Britain's army was small in 1933 when Hitler came to power it was because Churchill, as Chancellor of the Exchequer (1924–1929), along with most other people around the world, thought that a major new war would never come.

We tend to blame the framers of the Treaty of Versailles for the origins of war in 1939. But there is a good case (now growing in popularity) that instead blames the Great Depression of the 1930s, and the slump in many national economies from 1929 onwards, of which Germany was but one.

Look at the Nazi Party's votes before and after the Depression:

May 1928: 810,000 votes (2.6 per cent of the total)
September 1930: 6,409,600 votes (18.3 per cent of the total)
July 1932: 13,745,000 votes (37.3 per cent of the total)

All this is deeply significant. Before the slump, the Nazis were considered fringe lunatics. As the economic situation got worse, their vote went up – but it was still under twenty per cent in 1930. Only by 1932, when German politics were in chaos, did the Nazis gain significantly, and even then only just won over thirty-seven per cent of the vote.

What happened when the Crash of Wall Street began in October 1929 is that the USA recalled all its loans and ceased to subsidise the German economy. As the whole world then imploded financially, so too did Germany. And in that country, when things became hard, the German people began looking for scapegoats all around them for the disaster. Hitler, blaming the Jews and the German defeat in 1918, had as his audience a German people now ready to listen. By 1933 the Conservative Right, which had long since ceased to practise legitimate democratic politics, thought that if they made Hitler Chancellor of Germany that they could control him as their puppet. So Chancellor he became.

He was, as we know, no puppet. With President Hindenburg's death in 1934 Hitler became President of Germany as well, and thus the Führer with whom we are familiar.

But none of this was inevitable – it could all have been different.

So we can perhaps now say that the Treaty of Versailles in

1919, *combined with the effects of the Depression on Germany and the foolishness of non-Nazi reactionaries* put Hitler in power and then created the trajectory that lead to World War II.

And it is *now* that we can come to the traditional version: once Hitler was ruler of Germany, war became inevitable: Churchill was right.

(Churchill was out of office in 1933, not because he was anti-Hitler but because he zealously opposed independence for India. But for now that is another story . . .)

THE ORIGINS OF WORLD WAR II IN EUROPE: THE TRADITIONAL PERSPECTIVE

The sheer scale of the horror and carnage of World War I had alienated most decent West Europeans from ever having such a terrible war again. In retrospect we can see that appeasement with dictators such as Adolf Hitler or the Italian ruler Benito Mussolini, was a foolish move. We can see in hindsight that it would have been far better in 1936 or in 1938 to have stopped Hitler and maybe prevented World War II from ever happening.

(Our main emphasis in this chapter is on Germany, Britain's main enemy. But the United Kingdom also appeased Italy, over the latter's invasion of Ethiopia in 1935, and did not prevent either Germany or Italy from intervening in the civil war in Spain 1936–1939, in which Britain and France stayed officially neutral. And with Italy appeasement nearly worked! It was not until near the German conquest of France in 1940 that Italy actually joined Germany in fighting Britain, and the fascist dictator of Spain stayed neutral in relation to Britain and France throughout the war.)

But the key thing to remember is *that people at the time did not know what we know now*. Globally far more people were slaughtered in the Second World War than in the First, although in fact British deaths were to be fewer in the later war than they had been in the Somme or Western Front.

At the time though, people remembered the humungous losses of the trenches and felt, as we can understand, that they never wanted such a conflict ever again. What they did not realise of course is that Hitler wanted to have one, and that being nice to him, as British politicians tried to be after 1933, only made him far worse.

The other thing we overlook is that Britain and its Empire was financially broke in the 1930s. And up to 1967, in fact, the United Kingdom had global defence responsibilities that meant that in the crucial 1933–1939 period the British military chiefs were terrified of the consequences to Britain of a war simultaneously against Germany, Italy and Japan. By 1941 that is exactly what they got, but they spent those crucial pre-1939 years doing all possible to avoid precisely that contingency.

The other thing we forget is US isolationism. After 1941 the USA was more than fully engaged in the war and in 1945 – completely unlike 1918 – the US troops stayed in Europe rather than going home. But in the 1930s the American public wanted nothing to do with Europe and its Old World struggles. However sympathetic the President, Franklin D. Roosevelt, was to the cause of freedom, he was elected head of a nation that was firmly isolationist in its views. Churchill felt certain that the USA would one day come to the rescue. But it took the Japanese attack on Pearl Harbor in 1941 for this to happen. In 1938, the British Prime Minister, Neville Chamberlain, was far more representative of opinion in the United Kingdom when he said that the Americans were 'nothing but words'.

In retrospect the appeasement policy of the 1930s was a terrible tragedy, especially in the light of what happened afterwards. In 1938 came a real last chance to stop Hitler. Recent discoveries have shown that it was even more tragic than we knew at the time.

WAS WAR INEVITABLE?

The history of war is interesting. As we saw in *The Battles of World War I* historians are always changing their minds. This is true with accepted opinion about the origins of World War II, except that most people agree that Hitler was evil. The first version of the history of the war was Churchill's – the far-seeing and prophetic voice in the wilderness. He argued against appeasement and was proved right, in large measure not merely by events but by the books he wrote himself after the war.

Then came the revisionists, arguing that Churchill threw away the British Empire (which had been bankrupted by the Second World War). They said that this allowed the Americans to become the number one world power, and that appeasement was thus right after all.

Then finally come the neo-revisionists, who try to balance out the conflicting interpretations.

Obviously Hitler was a massive threat to world peace and to everything that decency and humanity holds dear. Churchill insisted on victory whatever the cost. Morally he was right. The idea of Hitler ruling an empire from the Atlantic Ocean to the Pacific (if he had conquered Britain in 1940 and the USSR in 1941) is too horrible to contemplate. We know now, for example, that he would have starved 40 million Russians to death as well as murdering all of Europe's Jews. Britain may indeed have lost the Empire, and let the USA instead of the United Kingdom rule the waves, but together we saved democracy and freedom and destroyed one of the most evil tyrannies that the world has ever seen.

MUNICH THE NEEDLESS TRAGEDY

All the arguments come together in 1938. Should we have defended Czechoslovakia, the one shining democracy in Central Europe, surrounded by a sea of despotic or quasi-dictatorial monarchies, and gone to war in October 1938? Or was it right to betray the Czechs, as Britain did in league with France and Italy, by signing the Munich Agreement with Hitler in 1938? This settlement gave him large chunks of Czech territory without a single German soldier needing to fight.

A brief recap: when the First World War ended the victorious allies created a series of multi-ethnic states such as Czechoslovakia and Yugoslavia, many of which no longer exist today. These contained within them many large ethnic minorities from the defeated powers. Many ethnic Germans lived in what is now the

Czech Republic and many Hungarians in present-day Slovakia. In February 1938 Hitler broke the Treaty of Versailles and reunited Germany with his Austrian homeland. Contrary to *The Sound of Music* story, most Austrians were overjoyed, since they were ethnically German. The poor Czechs now found themselves surrounded on three sides by a much bigger German Reich. And in all the Czech borderlands lived ethnic Germans – the Sudeten. But all of the main defences and munitions factories of Czechoslovakia were also in this region. War seemed imminent, as Hitler demanded that all the Sudeten part of Czechoslovakia be given to the Third Reich.

In terms of economics and defence capabilities, the British Chiefs of Staff were right that Britain could not possibly fight Germany, Italy and Japan at the same time. In 1941 it was only the entry of the USA (longed for by Churchill) that saved the day. So in terms of *what we knew* in 1938 the appeasers have a strong case, however immoral in hindsight. And as Churchill's wartime Chief of Staff Lord Ismay put it, what happened in 1938 was wrong, but *at that time* the overwhelming majority of Britons and Commonwealth countries, such as Canada and Australia, were resolutely *against* going to war. Never forget that when Chamberlain returned from Munich, having betrayed the Czechs by handing all their key defences and munitions and borders to Hitler, that massive cheering crowds in London praised him for avoiding a war.

What is tragic is that we now know that the USSR would have been willing to go to the aid of Czechoslovakia. Right up until late 1938 Joseph Stalin, the Soviet dictator, was open to a deal with the Western democracies to stop Hitler. But the British and

French politicians so hated the Soviet Union that not only were the poor Czechs excluded from the conference to partition their country at Munich but so too was the USSR. Again Churchill, a former anti-Bolshevik, now favoured a British–USSR alliance.

Stalin was furious. He sacked his Jewish Foreign Minister, Litvinov, who wanted to unite with the West against Hitler. He replaced him in 1939 with Molotov, a Stalin loyalist who was quite happy to deal with the Nazis direct in order to protect the USSR. So the true and massive tragedy of Munich was not simply the betrayal of the Czechs to Hitler, but the alienation of the USSR. As we shall see, Hitler and Stalin were to come together in August 1939, to the ruin of Western Europe. The Germans, unlike in World War I, would now only have to fight in the West, since they now had a treaty guarding them in the East, with the USSR. The whole nature of the war would change, to Hitler's advantage.

So in the short term the appeasers have a case. But long term they were horribly wrong, and that surely must be the verdict of history.

Therefore when Germany invaded Poland in late August 1939, the Nazis were able to partition that poor state with the Soviets, as we will see below. Britain now entered the war, but with the USSR neutral they were in a far worse position than would otherwise have been the case. Churchill was right.

But the war that started in September 1939 was in Europe only. The war was far bigger than that, so let us explore what we so often forget: it was to be a *global* conflict.

THE WAR THAT NEVER HAPPENED AND ITS CONSEQUENCES

And we forget too that Japan's original invasion plans included war against the USSR. If *that* had happened Stalin would have possibly faced a two-front war: against the Germans on the USSR's Western and European frontiers; and Japan on their Eastern and Asian frontiers. This might well have been a war that the Soviets could not have won.

But the pact with Hitler saved the Soviet Union in their Western border regions (Eastern Europe from a British/French perspective). And as we shall see, a key battle on the Mongolian/ Chinese border between the Soviet Red Army and Japanese forces determined an internal debate going on in China: should they go north against the USSR or south against the European and American colonies such as Vietnam, Malaysia, Indonesia and the Philippines? Japanese defeat determined the outcome: they would go *south* and risk inevitable war with the USA.

This changed the whole nature of the war. Stalin could relax with Japan until he chose to attack them after D-Day in Europe in 1945. Troops stationed in Siberia could be transferred to counter any German threat, as was to happen in 1941. A small battle near Mongolia changed the nature of the war and shows how interconnected the war with Japan was with that against Germany, thousands of miles away. The Japanese decision *not* to attack the USSR as well as the USA made a critical difference, as we shall see.

THE GLOBAL REACH OF WORLD WAR II

When we watch films about the war most of them, inevitably, concentrate on the battles against Germany in Western Europe or perhaps those fought slightly earlier against the Germans and Italians in North Africa. The exception would be American films set in the Pacific, in the war against the Japanese. But plenty of British, Australian and New Zealand forces also fought in the Pacific, and often in much harsher jungle terrain. Likewise, and this is a far bigger distortion, around eighty-five per cent of the Germans fought on the Eastern Front against the USSR. That means that only fifteen per cent of the German army was involved in fighting British and American troops in the Mediterranean and then in north-west Europe.

Television series such as *Band of Brothers* or films like *Saving*

Private Ryan do convey a wonderfully accurate view of what it must have been like to be an Allied soldier in 1944–1945. Films such as *The Guns of Navaronne* or *Charlotte Gray* ably demonstrate the bravery of those involved in clandestine war behind enemy lines and the moral dilemmas involved in such conflict.

But none of them show the major battles and battlefields of World War II. Only now, through television-documentary makers, do we know about the titanic struggles on the Eastern Front. Laurence Rees's programmes *World War II: Behind Closed Doors* and *War of the Century* provide excellent examples. Books by Norman Davies and Timothy Snyder have brought the kind of discussion, hitherto restricted to university history courses, to wider audiences. We all know about the Holocaust. But how many of us have heard of the Hunger Plan, the Nazi programme to starve forty million Soviet citizens to death? This is almost four times as many Russians and Ukrainians, for instance, as the ten million or so Jews in the whole of Europe whom the SS planned to kill if it had been given the chance.

World War II therefore is much wider and also far more ruthless and pernicious than most of us have realised. It was a war without the usual rules – the Germans regarded Slavs and Jews as subhuman. The Japanese regarded the Chinese in the same way, and with similar consequences. It was, in that sense, not just a conflict but an existential struggle, what historians now term 'total war', with civilians as well as soldiers involved in all aspects of the fighting.

MORAL AMBIGUITIES AND THE MYTH OF THE 'GOOD WAR'

As we saw the West tends to think of the Second World War as being a 'good war'. From a Western perspective, this is wholly understandable. Many people are still, 100 years later, debating whether or not World War I was a justifiable conflict. But the struggle against Hitler, and the vile Nazi ideology that he embodied, was a fight whose morality few would question.

As shown earlier, just before the outbreak of war in Europe, the USSR and the Third Reich were members of a neutrality pact that, for all intents and purposes, meant that Hitler and Stalin were allies August 1939–June 1941. The questionable morality of these two ruthless dictators, who soon were to fight on separate sides, led to unbelievable devastation. For it was, of course, Hitler who decided to break the neutrality pact and bring the Soviet

Union into the war in 1941 by invading them in Operation Barbarossa. That traitorous decision made the USSR Britain's uneasy ally against Germany. It also made the USSR and the USA partners after Hitler declared war on the USA in December of that year. The Soviet Union remained our co-belligerent until war ended in 1945.

Now that the USSR as such has not existed for over twenty years, there are many who do not remember or know what this Communist regime was like. It is reckoned that during his time in power (1922–1953) Stalin slaughtered twenty million of his own people in ideologically motivated mass murder. He had ordered the deaths of over three million innocent civilians even before war broke out in Europe in 1939.

As we have just seen, it was overwhelmingly Soviet Red Army soldiers who fought against the Germans in 1941–1945: Britain and the USA did not land in north-west Europe, on D-Day, until three years after the German invasion of the USSR had begun. But morally speaking, there was no real difference between Hitler and Stalin when it came to mass murder, ideological genocide and totalitarian horror. It was Red Army troops who liberated much of Central Europe, such as Poland, Hungary or the now former state of Czechoslovakia, from Nazi conquest. The problem for tens of millions of Poles, Hungarians, Czechs and others is that the Red Army simply exchanged one kind of tyranny for another. Not until 1989, forty-four years after VE-Day in 1945, did the Soviets finally leave and allow those countries the freedom and liberty that countries liberated by the British and Americans, such as France or the Netherlands, had enjoyed since the end of the war.

For a Pole, foreign rule started with the Nazi invasion in 1939 and lasted a full fifty years until the fall of the Iron Curtain in 1989. That is an experience of war very different from ours in the West. There is a moral ambiguity in the Second World War that gives it a profound double-edged feeling if we look at it in the context of the whole of Europe. It is more comfortable to forget this aspect of the war and to focus on the tales of the wonderfully courageous British, Commonwealth and American troops who fought from D-Day to VE-Day and to victory over the Germans.

Finally, one can suspect that while most British people are familiar with El Alamein, the United Kingdom/Commonwealth victory over German troops in late 1942, American readers will be less likely to know of this battle. By contrast, people in the USA might know of the great naval battles in the Pacific against the Japanese, such as Midway or Iwo Jima. British or Commonwealth readers may not be acquainted with them, even though in terms of the war against Japan they played as important a role as some of the battles after D-Day with which people on both sides of the Atlantic are very aware.

So as we go on to look at the battles of World War II, let us not forget the context in which we should see them. It was a truly global conflict and one that has shaped the world in which we live today ever since.

PART ONE

1937–1939

Prelude to War and Beginning Short

THE NANJING MASSACRE
(OR RAPE OF NANKING)

December 1937

As we saw earlier, one proposed starting date for World War II is July 7th 1937, when Chinese and Japanese troops began eight years of continuous warfare that lasted down to VJ-Day and the Japanese surrender in 1945.

The Japanese always referred to their war against China as an 'incident', but when their full-scale invasion of that country began it was a war, whatever its technical status. Shanghai fell swiftly to the invaders and then in December they attacked the former Chinese capital of Nanjing (then named Nanking). There the Chinese Nationalist Army surrendered virtually without a fight.

So the Japanese decided to massacre as many innocent men, women and children in the city as possible. The later

International Military Tribunal that investigated the slaughter estimated the death toll at 200,000 murdered, and the Chinese figure for the atrocity is 300,000 killed. Interestingly the Japanese figure is about 40,000, and the Japanese have never really owned up to the wide-scale carnage carried out by their troops. Tens of thousands of women were raped before being killed, and the Japanese army seems to have run amok. Even the German Embassy in its report was horrified at the sheer enormity of the crimes against humanity that the Japanese committed.

Because we start World War II in 1939 we forget that this atrocity took place. But since the Japanese have never acted to China as modern-day Germany has, for example, to Israel, it remains a source of acute tension between China and Japan right down to today.

Nanjing was only the start of a large-scale and eight-year-long campaign of atrocities committed by the Japanese on the Chinese people, with over twenty million of the latter slaughtered during that period. The attitude of the Japanese to the Chinese inhabitants was every bit as racist as the Germans' was to the Jews or Slavs, something we in the West often forget, but which the Chinese do not.

THE CONQUEST OF PRAGUE

March 16th 1939

Strictly speaking the occupation of Prague was a conquest, not a battle, as the Czechs decided not to fight the German invaders who took over their country in March 1939. For the Czechs it would be the start of a fifty-year nightmare since, apart from a brief spell of nominal freedom in 1945–1948, they were in effect to be under foreign domination, first under the Nazis and then under the Soviets. Finally, genuine liberty came with the Velvet Revolution against Communist oppression in late 1989.

How had it come to this? Czechoslovakia, as the country was named 1919–1939, was the beacon of democracy, freedom, and of Western civilisation and values in a region where dictatorship, anti-Semitic hatred and corruption was the norm. Bohemia and Moravia – what we now call the Czech Republic – had always been one of the most advanced, prosperous and tolerant parts of the old Austro-Hungarian Empire up until that county's demise in 1918. The new state, created out of that part of the old Austrian Empire, also included the mainly Slovak part of the old Kingdom of Hungary and a less developed part of Europe called Ruthenia, which since 1945 has been part of the Ukraine.

But it was an artificial creation, rather like the nation of Yugoslavia, which so dramatically and bloodthirstily imploded during World War II and again in the 1990s. For as well as the dominant Czechs, there were the Slovaks and Ruthenes, both also Slavic peoples. However, ethnic Germans were living in all of the mountain areas that surrounded the Czech parts of the country, in the regions bordering both Germany and Austria. Until 1918 they were content, since their overlord, the Austrian Emperor, was a German, like them. Come 1918 they found themselves an ethnic minority within a predominantly Slavic Czech/Slovak state, and they resented not being able to join their fellow Germans in either Austria or Germany.

Then in February 1938 Hitler conquered Austria, to the enormous enthusiasm and joy of most of the ethnically German-Austrian inhabitants. The Czech half of Czechoslovakia thus found itself surrounded by the Third Reich on three sides, a strategically very dangerous position.

Czechoslovakia was not only a liberal democracy that believed in freedom and the rule of law. It had, in the Skoda Works, the most advanced arms manufacturing capability that then existed in the world. The army was thus among the best-equipped anywhere in Europe. Not only that, but the Sudeten Mountain regions that bordered the new Third Reich provided some of the best natural defences available. It should have been impregnable, and this is just what the German military leaders in the Wehrmacht feared to be the case.

In addition, Czechoslovakia's territory had been guaranteed both by France and by the USSR. It is important to remember that back in 1939 there was no Soviet-Czech border, since Polish territory was then substantially in the way.

In 1938 Hitler wanted war, and the idea of reuniting the ethnic Germans living in Czechoslovakia gave him, he felt, the excuse for which he was looking.

Unfortunately this meant that in theory the French would have been obliged to come to Czechoslovakia's aid. So too would the Soviet Union, but the latter had the problem that no Polish government was going to allow Red Army troops through their territory in order to rescue the Czechs. And if France went to war with Germany it would have been impossible for the British to stand by and see the French in danger.

For the unfortunate Czechs this is where it all began to go wrong.

The British ruling elite was terrified of another world war. So many young men had been slaughtered on the Western Front (1914–1918) that for many in Britain it was a simple issue of 'never again'. Not only that but Britain was then a true world power, with vital strategic interests through the Mediterranean on to the vast imperial possessions in India and East Asia. Italy threatened the former and Japan the latter. Furthermore, the overwhelming view of the British military, as well as of the dominant political class, was that a war simultaneously against Germany, Italy and Japan was one that Britain could not possibly win.

Since the USA, the world's most powerful democracy, was locked away in what is called isolation, the British felt that they would have to fight any major wars without American help. Only Winston Churchill, a former government minister but now out of office and on the backbenches, thought otherwise.

Finally the British had considerably scaled down their armed forces, since to maintain an army, navy and air force of the size needed would, most people felt, bankrupt the country.

Thus came about the policy known as 'appeasement', of being nice to the dictators, and of giving way on demands that such hostile nations possessed that could be reasonably and rationally accommodated.

Morally speaking this was despicable, as Churchill never tired of pointing out. The Labour Party, the main Opposition, agreed with Churchill on disliking the dictators, but they put all their trust in peaceful negotiations and disliked the idea of rearmament – the only real way of making Britain safe enough to deal with the growing fascist/Nazi menace. Appeasement, therefore, was both immoral and the only logical way of avoiding war at the same time.

So, when Hitler began overtly to threaten Czechoslovakia in the summer of 1938, the British pressed the French into agreeing with appeasement rather than into preparing for war with Germany to defend the Czechs.

In September 1938 the crisis worsened and after much shuttle diplomacy by the British Prime Minister Neville Chamberlain, a meeting was convened in Munich, with Britain, France, Germany and Italy all present. The deal was struck on September 29th–30th, with Hitler signing for Germany. Almost all the Sudeten, or ethnically German parts of Czechoslovakia, were to be ceded to the Third Reich. This instantly denuded that county's natural defences, leaving it completely vulnerable to outside attack. The Czechoslovak government was faced with a *diktat* since they were not allowed to discuss their own fate. And, as we shall see, equally unfortunately the USSR, a state that had the right to guarantee Czechoslovakia's integrity, was also excluded, to Stalin's fury.

Theoretically Hitler promised that these were his final demands, since the rump of the country contained no ethnic Germans longing for reunion with their homeland. Hungary took the ethnically Hungarian parts of southern Slovakia and even the Poles participated in the dismemberment, annexing a disputed town to Poland.

Churchill was outraged, and some of the British government resigned. But Chamberlain was cheered as he waved to the delighted crowds from the balcony of Buckingham Palace. The overwhelming sensation in Britain was that the country had been spared war and that Chamberlain was the man who had rescued the nation from certain carnage. There would be no more battles like that of the Somme in 1916 in which the British and Empire forces lost 57,000 on the first day alone. Nor did the key Dominions, such as Canada and Australia, want war either, and in those days their views carried considerable weight.

Then on March 16th 1936 Hitler changed everything.

The rump Czech half was annexed to the Third Reich as the Protectorate of Bohemia and Moravia. Slovakia became a nominally independent state under the control of local fascists, and Ruthenia, after a single day as a country of its own, was annexed by Hungary (and by the USSR in 1945). The Czechs were not Germans, and so there was no excuse now that Hitler was simply reuniting the divided members of the German race.

Suddenly and rather late the British government woke up to the fact that Hitler could not after all be trusted, and that war was now inevitable whether Britain wanted it or not. Chamberlain introduced conscription (which in the previous war had not been ordered until 1916) and began to put out feelers to countries that might want to be protected from Nazi invasion. Churchill had been vindicated completely, but it would not be until war itself broke out on September 3rd that he was actually allowed back into the government.

Appeasement and the Munich settlement have been argued about ever since. Britain did end up, by 1941, fighting Germany, Italy and Japan, and did also go bankrupt. But in December 1941, as we shall see, Churchill's dreams came true and the USA entered the war and rescued the United Kingdom. For Chamberlain the Americans were 'nothing but words'. But when war did break out Roosevelt, as Churchill expected, did everything he could to help the British from being defeated by Nazi Germany, short, as he put it, 'of war itself'.

When Britain and the Dominions did go to war in September 1939 it was as a united country and united British Empire. From March 1939 onwards everyone knew it was bound to happen, that the Nazis were as evil as painted and that Hitler had to be stopped.

German generals captured during the war confessed that had Britain and France gone to war in September 1938 – a year earlier – with the Czechs resisting fully behind their natural defences and state-of-the-art army, Germany would have found it very difficult indeed to win. And the argument, by Chamberlain's apologists, that Munich gave the British an extra year to rearm, is contradicted by the fact that it also gave the Germans a year to rearm as well. Not only that, but as the Skoda Works were captured by Germany in March 1939, the Third Reich now had the best armaments factory in Europe.

Furthermore, since the Czechs felt it was futile to resist, all the weapons of the Czechoslovakian army fell into German hands. When France was invaded in 1940, it was magnificent Czech tanks and military hardware that the Wehrmacht was able to employ *against* the Allies, rather than would have been the case in 1938, on the Allied side.

However, in September 1938 the British, along with nations such as Canada, New Zealand and Australia, were not ready for war. In September 1939 everybody was ready to fight. But the price paid – the savage betrayal to Nazi Germany of the great Czechoslovak democracy – was a hideous one. And as the Poles, who had stolen Czech territory in 1938, were now to discover, Britain was in no position to help them militarily and there was a profoundly angry Stalin wondering what next to do.

THE BATTLES OF KHALKHIN GOL

May–September 1939

Khalkhin Gol is an obscure region of what is now Mongolia, but near the border with China. In 1939 some clashes took place there close to the village of Nomonhan, between the Japanese Kwantung Army and those of the Soviet Red Army that some say altered the course of the entire Second World War.

Search in some books and you will see no reference at all to the skirmishes that happened in May–August, or even to the major battle in August 20th–31st between the Japanese and the Red Army, with the Soviet forces under the command of General Georgii Zhukov, who would go on to be one of the most famous soldiers of World War II. However, academic writers such as Evan Mawdsley and famous historians such as Antony Beevor have now given the battle of August 1939 its proper due. And if they

are right, then, by giving the Soviet Red Army so overwhelmingly decisive a victory against the Japanese, it completely changed the nature of the whole war. This includes those of us in Britain and the USA, for whom the USSR's survival against Hitler in 1941 was the turning point that helped us to beat both the Germans and the Japanese in 1945.

Let us go back to the options for the Japanese in 1936, if we are to understand why a clash between just a few thousand soldiers in a place 350 miles from the nearest railway station made such an impact on the war.

In 1936 the Japanese had signed the Anti-Comintern (anti-Communist) Pact with Nazi Germany and their then Prime Minister Koki Hirota had declared that Japan's greatest threat lay from the USSR.

That continued to be the case so far as many in Japan were concerned. However another faction in Japan wanted to get as much oil as possible because of the danger that such supplies would be cut off as a result of Japan's other policy, war against China. As we have just seen, this began in earnest in 1937, and the Americans, who had close ties to China, were furious. If the USA embargoed oil being delivered from the then oil-rich Dutch East Indies (now Indonesia), for example, then the Japanese would have no choice but to get their supplies by force.

As Ian Kershaw points out in *Fateful Choices*, this action would have inevitably lead to war with the USA, since they would never have tolerated a Japanese invasion of East Asia. The decision would lead to Pearl Harbor, the Japanese attack on the US fleet in Hawaii and the eventual defeat of Japan in 1945. This course of events was known as the *southern option*.

But others in Japan believed in another choice – the *northern option.*

Japanese troops had in fact briefly attacked the infant USSR after the Bolshevik Revolution in 1917. And in 1904–1905 the Japanese had utterly humiliated Tsarist Russia in a war fought in East Asia, with the famous naval victory at Tsushima.

For many Japanese leaders up until 1939, war against the Soviet Union remained a real possibility. However, in August 1939, when General Georgii Zhukov was placed in charge of the Red Army forces in eastern Siberia – along the borders of Mongolia and of Japanese-ruled Manchukuo – things changed. The Soviets had become fed up with Japanese military pinpricks and provocations. So on August 20th Red Army troops under his command, acting in tandem with Red Air Force planes in full tactical support, attacked the Japanese Kwantung Army forces. An entire Japanese division was both surrounded and destroyed. On August 31st the fighting stopped and on September 15th Japan agreed a ceasefire.

Accounts differ enormously on the casualties. But the most reliable reckon that about 10,000 Red Army troops were killed or missing and 25,000 Japanese forces suffered the same fate.

This was a disaster for Japan. The *northern option* was effectively cancelled, although it reappeared in the minds of some as a possibility after the German invasion of the USSR in June 1941.

But the fact that the Japanese did not join with the Italians, Spanish, Romanians and Hungarians in supporting Germany in Barbarossa in attacking the Soviet Union is significant. On April 13th 1941 the Soviets and Japanese signed a non-aggression pact, to which Japan adhered strictly, as did the USSR until they declared war against the Japanese in 1945, after victory in Europe against Germany had been assured.

The Pacific War of 1941–1945, with Pearl Harbor in 1941 and the Japanese conquest of Singapore and other European-ruled colonies in Asia in 1942, is relatively familiar to readers of history. It is less well known that the Japanese had another choice. Indeed many good books ignore that factor altogether, since what happened seems so obvious to us.

However they could have taken another road – which was stopped at Khalkhin Gol. Zhukov was to go on to rescue Moscow from the Germans in December 1941 and be in charge of the victorious capture of Berlin in May 1945. He is regarded as one of the best commanders of World War II. His victory at Khalkhin Gol consolidated his reputation as a military genius.

But one could argue that it was his 1939 victory over Japan that really saved his country. What made all the difference between victory and defeat for the USSR in December 1941, when a large German army was at the gates of Moscow, was that thousands of battle-hardened Red Army troops could be safely removed from Siberia to rescue the Soviet capital from what seemed like inevitable doom. All this was only possible, though, because Stalin knew that the Japanese had now embarked on war with the USA that month, and would not invade Russia from the east. He would only have to fight on one front – against the Germans. Not until after Hitler's death would the USSR join Britain and the USA in fighting Japan.

There is little doubt that had Stalin been obliged to fight a two-front war in 1941 – against the Germans from the West and the Japanese from the East – then the USSR could not possibly have survived. In which case the Axis Powers would have scored a massive victory, and maybe even won the war, or at least elongated it by many years. Japan though would also have had to fight a two-front war – against the USSR in Siberia and the USA in the Pacific – and been even more overstretched than they were already, just fighting Britain and the USA.

Either way, a Japanese victory at Khalkhin Gol and a Japanese link up with the Germans in 1941 over Barbarossa would have led to a very different and far more bloodthirsty war than even the one that actually happened. Zhukov's victory, in so clear a manner, stopped all such possibilities. Japan came to understand in 1939, as Germany failed to do in 1941, how formidable an opponent the Red Army would be. A battle few have heard of and in a place hundreds of miles from anywhere really did make a major difference to the outcome of the whole Second World War.

THE BATTLE FOR POLAND

September 1st–October 6th 1939

The battle to conquer Poland was the opening of the Second World War in Europe. It is remembered today mainly for triggering British and French entry into the war on September 3rd 1939, the day familiar to most people in the West as the outbreak of conflict. Poland was invaded on September 1st by Germany from the west and on September 17th by the Soviet Union from the east. Being attacked on two fronts and with no natural defences (in that sense very unlike Czechoslovakia), it did not take long to conquer Poland.

There are two things to consider here. First, what happened to Poland and secondly what was Nazi Germany doing to act in harmony with the Communist USSR? The first affected just Poland but the other factor made a huge difference to the whole war.

The German invasion may be familiar to most readers, but how many remember that Poland had two enemies in 1939? Poles bitterly refer to this dual invasion as the 'fourth partition of Poland'. To understand why this country was invaded on both sides we need to look at some previous history. For the Poles had the tragic experience of being surrounded by enemies.

Up until the eighteenth century Poland was one of the largest countries in Europe, then encompassing much of today's Lithuania, Belarus and Ukraine as well as the region we think of as Polish today. However, its predatory neighbours – Russia, Prussia (the core state of what became Germany) and the Austrian empire carved it up into three divisions, wiping it from the map until Poland was finally restored in 1918. But in its victory the Poles took lots more territory than were ethnically Polish – in 1939 there were large Belarus and Ukrainian minorities, as well as one of the biggest Jewish populations in Europe.

In the Polish–Soviet war in 1918–1920 the Poles had easily bested the infant Red Army troops, to the humiliation of one of the latter's commissars, a certain Joseph Stalin. Up until 1938 Stalin had been happy to go along with the idea of an anti-fascist front, with the Soviet Foreign Minister, Maxim Litvinov, who was also Jewish, in charge of the attempt to create one. But the deliberate exclusion of the USSR from the Munich talks that split up Czechoslovakia had, understandably, enraged Stalin. Litvinov was sacked and was replaced by the ethnically Russian Vyacheslav Molotov.

Stalin now distrusted the Western leaders, such as Neville Chamberlain, as much as they were wary of him. Attempts by Britain and France to bring the USSR into an anti-Nazi alliance were half-hearted on both sides. More important, the Poles were profoundly distrustful of the USSR, and with good cause as a result of the 1918–1920 war. They refused any permission for Red Army troops to cross into their territory to fight Hitler, and as Britain put its relations with Poland first, that ended any realistic hopes of a British–Soviet defence deal.

But Hitler had no scruples in negotiating directly with Stalin, and he could do something that the British could not – restore to the USSR the territory lost to Poland in 1920.

Part of Hitler's own core belief was a hatred of Communism which, conflated with his visceral anti-Semitism, led to a hatred of what he described as Jewish-dominated Bolshevism. This was all nonsense, as Stalin was not above being anti-Semitic himself. Up until August 1939 anti-Bolshevism had appeared to be at the heart of German policy as well. Suddenly it was Adolf Hitler, the most rabid anti-Communist, reaching out in a deal with the Soviet Union! The two foreign ministers, Ribbentrop for Germany and Molotov for the USSR, worked out the details and, as a result, the Nazi-Soviet Pact, signed on August 23rd 1939 in Moscow, is often called the Molotov-Ribbentrop Pact as a result.

Ideologically it was indeed astonishing! But both of the dictators had strong reasons for their strange actions. For Hitler it meant that he could attack the USSR at a time of his choosing – as he was to do in June 1941. He would therefore be fighting a war on one front only, on the West, and could concentrate his offensive resources for that conflict. For Stalin, well aware of the deficiencies of the Red Army – caused in large part by his paranoid purges of much of the officer corps – he would be given valuable time to build up defences. And ideologically the idea of the capitalist powers fighting each other to pieces while the Communists could look on and take future advantage was for him powerful as well.

Not only that but in the secret codicils to the agreement, eastern Poland would become part of the USSR, while Germany seized the western half of the country. The Baltic States would also come under Soviet predominance, and the USSR was to snuff out the independence of the three Baltic nations in 1940, with their independence not restored until 1991.

Stalin thought he had a deal – only to find he did not come June 1941, as we shall see.

For the Poles, the double invasion was catastrophic, and for the enormous Jewish population it would be the beginning of the killing part of what we now call the Holocaust, the deliberate racial genocide of millions of Jews at the hands of the Third Reich.

By 1945 as many Poles were to be slaughtered as Jews throughout Europe. The Red Army and Stalin's secret police the NKVD were to prove a match in terror for the SS, something that we are only now coming to realise in the West, thanks to excellent documentaries by Laurence Rees and by the books of Norman Davies and Timothy Snyder. In August 1939 it was Stalin, not Hitler, who had already butchered countless innocent lives, with over three million people murdered in the Ukraine during the purges and political persecutions of the 1930s. At a remote forest location near the village of Katyn (in the same region as the town of Smolensk), the NKVD murdered some 22,000 Polish officers, a war crime well remembered in Poland to this day, but denied by the Soviet Union well into the 1990s.

The brief Polish war is remembered for two things, sadly neither being true. The Poles still had a cavalry corps, but the legend that brave Polish lancers attacked German tanks is regrettably untrue. And while the invasion of Poland is correctly remembered for the German *blitzkrieg* (literally 'lightening war'), what utterly destroyed Poland was the fact that they had not reckoned on being attacked from two sides, from the USSR as well as Germany. The intrepid Poles were caught between two giants, and it is amazing that as many Polish soldiers were able to escape – and fight courageously alongside British soldiers in Italy and north-west Europe – without being massacred by both the Wehrmacht and Red Army invaders.

Poland was not much of a democracy. It was a quasi-military dictatorship, and, as we just saw, a country quite happy to join Nazi Germany in stealing parts of Czechoslovakia in 1938. But it was a bulwark against both the horrors of Nazism on one side and of Stalinist rule on the other. Well over five million Poles were to die by 1945, and it would not be until 1989 that true freedom – with democracy added this time – was restored to the Polish people.

PART TWO: I

1939–1941
Early War: Western Europe

THE WINTER WAR: USSR VS FINLAND

November 30 1939–March 13 1940

How many people realise that Finland and the Soviet Union were at war with each other while the rest of Europe either was at war with Germany or was imminently in fear of being invaded?

In the West we tend to forget the period of August 1939–June 1941, during which the USSR and Third Reich were effectively allies. We have just seen this in the chapter on Poland, but with Finland it would be different.

The Finns, not unlike the Poles, spent centuries ruled by other nations, in their own case mainly by Sweden, but more importantly by Russia 1809–1917. Finland had gained its full independence in 1918, but its position, like those of the three Baltic States (Estonia, Latvia and Lithuania) was always precarious.

The Soviets wished to regain as much of the lost territories of 1917–1918 as possible, and also to build a bulwark under their direct control as a possible buffer against German expansion, should Hitler break his word.

In theory, in October 1939, the Soviets simply asked the Finns for some territorial adjustments and the right to use the Finnish (but pre-1917 Russian) naval base at Hasko. But as Stalin also put in place a dummy Soviet-controlled Finnish government-in-waiting, it was clear to the Finns that the USSR meant to conquer them. They therefore refused all Soviet requests, and were duly attacked by the Red Army on November 30th.

If Stalin and his forces had thought that the overwhelming odds against the Finns would make the latter a pushover, they were profoundly mistaken. Natural defences favoured the Finnish defenders, and the Mannerheim Line (named after their hero of independence and president) proved a strong bulwark against the attackers.

In the end the sheer weight of numbers told, and in March the Finns were obliged to surrender. They were not conquered outright, however, but did lose territory to the USSR (still held by Russia today) and they had to concede the port of Hasko as well. The Finns lost 50,000 but the Red Army losses were well over 100,000, which as historians remind us is more than all the German Wehrmacht losses in the whole of 1939–1940 inclusive. It was a heavy price to pay.

British and French sympathy was entirely with the Finns. Extraordinarily both Britain and France actually thought of going to war with the USSR to defend the Finns. This would have involved breaching the neutrality of three countries – Sweden and Norway in Scandinavia and that of Turkey. The last was involved because the Allies planned to bomb and destroy the Baku oil fields – the USSR's main source of vital petrol supplies to Germany under the Nazi–Soviet Pact. The Turks wisely refused the Allies overflight rights, so Baku was never attacked. And Finland surrendered just before both Allied and Nazi plans came into effect to invade Norway, as we shall now see.

There is little doubt that war with the USSR as well as with Nazi Germany would have been disastrous for the Allies, and as France itself fell in June 1940 the issue was never raised again. In June 1941 Hitler's decision to invade the USSR made the Soviets allies of the British, so it is just as well that actual Russo-British-French hostilities had never broken out in 1939–1940.

In June 1941 the Finns, foolishly but understandably, allied with the Third Reich in Barbarossa, the invasion of the USSR. While they temporarily regained some territory, they lost their gains once more when Germany was defeated. But the memory of the stout Finnish resistance meant that, unlike so many countries in Central Europe, Finland was allowed to be a democracy after 1945, albeit under Soviet oversight and the attendant restrictions. With the fall of the Iron Curtain in 1991 full Finnish independence and freedom of action was restored, a tribute to Finnish bravery in 1939–1940.

THE NORWEGIAN CAMPAIGN

April 9th–June 10th 1940

Whoever controls Norway can control much or all of the North Sea. And this was something that both the British and the Germans both came to realise in 1940. In addition, Sweden, while a neutral country, exported vast amounts of its iron ore riches to Germany, and most of that material came via the Norwegian ports by ship to the Reich.

Norway in April 1940 was neutral, as it had been in the First World War. But Winston Churchill, as First Lord of the Admiralty, realised that as so much vital war material was coming to Germany via Norway, that the Norwegian coastal waters would have to be mined to prevent German ships from getting through. This was a complete breach of Norwegian neutrality, but the British, who like their French ally were still relying heavily on economic means to defeat Germany, felt that it was worth the risk.

Simultaneously many in Germany felt it necessary to occupy Norway to prevent just such an event from taking place. If the Germans conquered Norway they could also safely control much of the North Sea. They had planned this in detail as early as January 1940. What made their plan interesting was that it was triphibious – with army, navy and air force all acting in combination and in a way that it took the Allies some time to emulate.

Norway was thus attacked on April 9th 1940, and the use of parachute troops and the Luftwaffe took the Norwegians completely by surprise. The Royal Navy, under Churchill's political command, failed to prevent the capture of the key port of Trondheim, but were temporarily successful in seizing Narvik, further to the north.

The Royal Navy has been strongly criticised for its lack of co-ordination in defending Norway – the official historian Captain Stephen Roskill was especially stern on Churchill's attempts to micromanage the action. But while this is true in relation to the Norwegian campaign itself, the Kriegsmarine (or German navy) suffered major losses that set German naval capabilities back for months. Crucially, as historians such as Ewan Mawdsley have reminded us, this meant that in the autumn of 1940 the German Navy was in no shape to help with the planned invasion of Britain – Sealion. That in turn enabled the Royal Navy to enjoy total command of the North Sea during the all-important period of the Battle of Britain. It was as much naval supremacy in September–October 1940 that rescued Britain from invasion as the brave fighter pilots in the skies.

The performance of British troops in Norway proved disastrous – all the best soldiers were either in training or in France. The army had to be evacuated ignominiously from their positions in Norway as they soon would be from Dunkirk.

One of the ironies of the Norwegian campaign is that the politician in charge, Winston Churchill, was to be the main beneficiary. The House of Commons was furious at the debacle and there was a motion of no confidence in Chamberlain's government. In the debate of May 7th–8th Churchill did all possible to defend both himself and the Prime Minister, but the government's theoretically impregnable majority plummeted. It became obvious that while the immediate disaster was Churchill's, in reality only Churchill, presiding over a genuinely multi-party wartime coalition, could lead Britain to victory.

On May 10th 1940 Churchill thus became Prime Minister. But it is not an event we can take for granted. Many on both sides of the House wanted the Foreign Secretary Lord Halifax. Had the latter become Prime Minister instead, we could well have had a peace deal with Hitler, especially after the fall of France not long later, and we would have lost the war. There were many who would have been open to such a treacherous deal, and Churchill had to work hard to keep his government colleagues on his side when he argued that Britain had to keep on fighting whatever the cost. British survival in 1940 was hideously close, much more so than we now take for granted.

Furthermore, as Paul Kennedy, the British historian at Yale University has pointed out, Churchill always wanted to go back to Norway to liberate the country to make up for his failure in 1940. But as all his military advisers told him regularly, Operation Jupiter would have been logistically highly dangerous and possibly very costly. It therefore never happened. But until the end of the war, Hitler kept 400,000 German troops on guard in Norway just in case the British (and later Americans) did try such an invasion. All those troops were entirely useless, ready for a non-existent attack. And that also means that they were unavailable to fight the Allies in north-west Europe or in Italy: 400,000 German forces whom the Allies never had to overcome. Jupiter may never have happened, but Hitler's suspicion that Churchill wanted to redeem the 1940 debacle surely saved thousands of Allied lives, especially after 1944.

DUNKIRK AND THE FALL OF FRANCE

May 10th–June 25th 1940

The fall of France, in the German *blitzkrieg* of May–June 1940 is one of the most debated issues in history. (This chapter takes it from the invasion of May 10th to the effective Armistice on June 25th – other publications may give different dates.) And the evacuation of the British Expeditionary Force from the beaches of Dunkirk has become part of British national folklore.

In one sense, the French defeat is not surprising. Germany (or its forerunner states) invaded France three times: in 1870, 1914 and in 1940. Germany won two out of those three times, and it was only by the narrowest of margins that the French succeeded in stopping the German advance in 1914. Luck probably played a large part in that particular escape.

Much of the debate is political, and to do with the fact that

French society in the 1930s was highly divided. Many French people were far more afraid of Stalin than Hitler, and since that was true of millions all across Europe they were by no means alone in that sentiment. In addition, the French had, one could argue, learnt the wrong lessons from their hideous losses in 1914–1918. Like the Chinese in ancient times, who built the vast Great Wall to keep out the barbarians, the French after 1918 had put their trust in a long line of fortifications known as the Maginot Line. Unfortunately for them, as for the medieval Chinese, they had an enemy who was much smarter and knew how to get around the defences and attack their foe at their weakest spot.

However, historians are right to say that French military thinking was not entirely defensive in nature. While far too much of France's army was bottled up in fortresses on the Maginot Line, others were ready to take the fight to the enemy should Hitler's troops take the same route as the German army in 1914. Some of the key French forces were thus ready to attack the invaders on the line of the River Dyle in Belgium. The British Expeditionary Force, under the command of General Lord Gort (a holder of the VC from World War I) also aimed to help their French allies in what they felt would be a key battle.

September 1939–May 1940 is known appropriately as the 'phoney war', a phrase coined by American Senator William Borah, about the fact that although Britain and France were at war with the Third Reich they did, in effect, nothing about it on the Western Front, where all the action had been in 1914–1918. There were plenty of ideas for diversions, such as fighting in the Balkans or, as we saw, against the Soviet Union to protect Finland. But apart from one very brief French excursion into German soil, the Allies took no offensive action against the territory of the Reich. They depended wholly instead on what is called 'economic warfare', on aiming to blockade Germany, and on avoiding the casualties of the previous war.

While the wish to avoid another Battle of the Somme is understandable, the lack of fighting spirit does in retrospect seem quite extraordinary. It embodied the cautious approach both of the French and of Neville Chamberlain, the British Prime Minister. Needless to say it infuriated Winston Churchill, who had been First Lord of the Admiralty (in charge of the Royal Navy) since September 1939. It was perhaps just as well for everyone that on May 10th 1940, when the Germans began their invasion of France, Churchill became Prime Minister and able to take the struggle against Hitler seriously.

The Germans did send troops that conquered both the Netherlands (which had been neutral in World War I) and Belgium, conquering both nations in five days of *blitzkrieg*, combining a ground invasion of men and tanks with an airborne attack of devastating power from the Luftwaffe against Belgian and Dutch cities. This is where the Allies expected them.

But the Germans were in effect deceiving them. General Erich von Manstein had a brilliant plan. Group B was attacking where anticipated, in the Low Countries. But Group A, the main German invasion, would be through the forest of the Ardennes, which the French had not bothered to defend properly as they deemed it impossible for an invading force to penetrate. Their troops guarding the Ardennes area were all second class and suddenly, to the horror of France, these inferior troops found themselves up against the cream of the German invading forces.

To Manstein this was the 'sickle cut' strategy: to ram through the barely defended Ardennes and cut off the British and French troops up on the Belgian border.

So successful was the plan that the German forces, many under the command of the dashing Panzer General Heinz Guderian and another risk-taking officer, Erwin Rommel, that they were able to achieve an astonishing 150 miles from their starting point on the River Meuse in just five days. On May 20th they had reached the coast, completely cutting off the key French armies and the entire British Expeditionary Force. Not only that but the French now had no reserves – all of them were either isolated in Belgium or locked up in the Maginot Line fortresses.

The situation of the British was now impossible. They had thought that they could try to link up with other French forces in the fight against the Germans, but as the sickle cut had isolated them totally their only option was to retreat ignominiously back to the United Kingdom.

Here the British genius for improvisation came to their rescue. Operation Dynamo (May 26th–June 4th) was an extraordinary success. No fewer than 340,000 Allied troops (of which around 100,000 were French) were evacuated from the beaches of Dunkirk safely back to Britain. While the overwhelming majority were taken back in Royal Navy ships, what took the imagination were the thousands of soldiers who were ferried across the English Channel in little boats – trawler ships, fishing boats, pleasure craft – by brave civilians determined to do their bit to help.

This was to make a vast difference to British wartime survival, since without those forces the United Kingdom would have been far more vulnerable to invasion. But the cost was still very high. Some 30,000 British troops had to stay behind and were taken prisoner. Most of the equipment was also abandoned on the beaches, and all that was not evacuated fell into German hands. As Churchill was right to point out, wars are not won by evacuations.

The British evacuation had been aided by a two-day German army halt near by. Conspiracy theorists have spun all sorts of tales about the reasons, most of which imply that Hitler let the British escape in order better to negotiate a peace deal with them at his time of choosing. But there is not the remotest evidence for this, and the real reason is almost certainly more prosaic: a pause to re-equip for the German Panzer Divisions before going on, as they anticipated, to defeat the French.

France continued the now forlorn struggle for a few more weeks, with Churchill doing all he could to give the increasingly defeatist French government as much moral courage and support as possible. One young general, Charles de Gaulle, became Under Secretary for War, and also did his best to give some fighting spirit to his fellow countrymen.

But it was proving a vain task. De Gaulle had to flee to Britain to start a resistance movement from London. On June 16th the former World War I hero Marshal Pétain, now eighty-four years old, was put in charge of France. He decided that the situation was hopeless. Hitler summoned the French government to the railway carriage at Compiègne, where the Germans had surrendered to the Allies back in 1918. The Armistice was signed on June 22nd. A nominally independent French state in southern France, based at the spa town of Vichy, was allowed to continue, while Germany occupied all the key northern and Atlantic regions of France direct.

German casualties were around 27,000 dead and British deaths were under 3,000. France lost over 100,000 dead, some 200,000 wounded and around 1.5 million French troops were taken prisoner. For Germany it would prove a relatively cheap victory, but for France the psychological blow was horrific.

And as Churchill told the House of Commons in London, the battle for France was now over but the battle for Britain was now about to begin . . .

THE BATTLE OF BRITAIN

July 10th–October 31st 1940

If one watches television news or documentaries they are full of 'battles that changed the war'. As we shall see in the battles described in this book, many of them were important, not a few made a long-term difference, and some also greatly enhanced the morale of the side that won that particular episode. But very few battles could actually claim significantly to have changed the outcome of the whole war.

The Battle of Britain, fought mainly over the skies of the eastern side of England in the late summer/early autumn of 1940, was genuinely one of those key moments that made a crucial difference between victory and defeat. It really was that important. Not only was it critical, but also won by the narrowest of hairsbreadths possible, and shows how extraordinarily close

Britain came to be conquered by the Nazis. The dates above are those of the Air Ministry, but in reality the battle was from 'Eagle Day' (August 13th) to Hitler's decision to postpone the invasion indefinitely on September 17th.

In Continental Europe, outside of the vastness of the USSR, the German *blitzkrieg* tactics seemed, for many years, to be utterly invincible. A combination of Panzer tanks with elite ground forces and proper co-ordination with the Luftwaffe fighters and bombers seemed, for the Third Reich, a winning formula. The one time that the British had to face such a mix, in northern France in 1940, saw an ignominious defeat and a quick scuttle back across the English Channel.

But then came the crucial difference.

Britain is of course an island, so the normal *blitzkrieg* employed by the Germans would not work unless they were able to cross the channel in such numbers that their usual show of sudden and overwhelming force would crush a defending British land army.

Many British writers, from the distinguished author Richard Holmes, familiar to television audiences, and others such as Gordon Corrigan, have rightly lambasted the successive British governments of the 1920s and 1930s for not building up an enormous land army capable of taking on the armed might of Nazi Germany. It is easy to sympathise with them, and in many ways they are right.

But in retrospect, those like Winston Churchill, who spent much of the 1930s arguing instead for a massive increase in the size of the Royal Air Force, had a case as well. In the past, anyone conquering Britain needed complete control of the sea, and the

Royal Navy was able to keep its superiority over the German fleet in the North Sea.

This meant that to land German troops on British soil the Nazis had to have *control of the air*; this they believed they had, especially since, after the fall of France in June 1940, they were able to use French airbases from which to attack English cities and RAF bases.

But thankfully successive British governments had realised that air power was a vital key to defence. Consequently, the Fighter Command of the RAF, under its taciturn and not always convivial commander, Air Chief Marshal Sir Hugh Dowding, had *just* enough planes left to put up a real fight against the German Luftwaffe invaders. And the former World War I air ace, Herman Goering, in charge of the invasion plans, was more bluster than skill.

Several things helped to save the British. This is the time when Churchill's inspired leadership began to make a difference, and his appointments, such as that of the Canadian press baron Lord Beaverbrook as Minister for Aircraft Production gave dynamism to a vital industry at a key time. The Luftwaffe had suffered heavy losses in the Battle for France. Hitler, while announcing Sealion, the code name for the invasion of Britain, dithered for two vital months while expecting Britain to surrender and strike a deal, similar to the one he had struck with Philippe Pétain in France. He could not quite believe that a fellow Nordic race would continue to wish to oppose him, but, thanks to Churchill, such was indeed the case. As a result, historians reckon that the RAF was able to increase its air force over those critical two months of delay, until the airborne invasion began in earnest in August.

And the British were not alone! This is a great myth. The RAF in particular had no fewer than thirteen different nationalities among its pilots, from expected places such as the Empire (Australia, Canada, New Zealand, South Africa) but also volunteers from the USA (still a neutral country) and from escaped pilots with superb combat experience, especially 145 from Poland and 88 from Czechoslovakia. Given the closeness of the air battles, and that much of the fighting has correctly been called an aerial war of attrition, such pilots made the all-important difference in the margin between success and failure.

In July 1940 there were 1,100 German fighters against just 700 for the RAF. It did not look good. But the British planes – the now legendary Spitfires and Hurricanes – showed that technical superiority could make up for a great deal of numeric inferiority. Radar, which gave the British the ability to know where the enemy was coming from, made defence much easier, and while ULTRA (the ability to break the German military codes) was still in its infancy, it certainly helped give much needed information about the enemy as well.

Patrick Bell has called the period August 13th–September 6th the 'crux of the battle'. On August 15th the Germans lost twice as many planes as the RAF, which turned out just as well, since between August 8th–18th the British had lost no fewer than 154 pilots killed or injured, and, just as vitally, as many as 231 planes. Now the Germans were taking the sensible steps of bombing the radar stations – thus blinding the British on where the Luftwaffe was – and also the RAF Fighter Command Sector Stations, the bases from whence came all the commands to the pilots on where they should be flying. On August 31st the RAF lost thirty-nine planes in a single day. The situation of the war of attrition was not looking promising.

Then a stroke of luck came the British way. Some German bombs had hit suburban London on August 24th–25th. Churchill thus ordered a retaliatory raid on Berlin, which turned out to be rather a damp squib. But so enraged was Hitler that the RAF had even dared to attack the German capital that, to a hysterical crowd on September 4th he ordered an overwhelming air raid on London.

On September 7th 1940 a mammoth bombing campaign was unleashed upon London. Many Londoners nicknamed this 'the Blitz', which is what it has been called ever since. Technically *blitzkrieg* is lightening war, of the kind that defeated Poland or the Netherlands in just a few days. But 'Blitz', even if inaccurate, has stuck.

Hundreds of bombers over two nights killed 400 Londoners, and injured thousands more, nearly all civilians. As someone observed, not since 1666 and the Great Fire of London had the capital seen such a scorching blaze.

But while it might have satisfied Hitler's ego, strategically it was a gigantic mistake. Fighters were needed to escort the bombers, so the Luftwaffe was no longer employing them to destroy radar stations or control centres. The RAF was now able to recoup in a way that had seemed impossible before the raids on London.

For on September 15th the RAF was able to rise up and wreak havoc against the incoming enemy bomber crews. The RAF lost twenty-six planes, and the Germans sixty. The British and their allies had achieved air superiority and the invasion would now be impossible. On September 30th the Luftwaffe lost forty-eight aircraft, the RAF just twenty; to many people that meant that the Battle of Britain was in effect over.

(Officially it ended on October 31st and one could say that the cancellation of Sealion on September 17th is equally a good conclusion, as that was the day when invasion was postponed, never in fact to take place.)

Why was all this so important?

Churchill had decided in May 1940, with the support of his government, to continue the fight. His advisers such as General Sir Alan Brooke, in 1940 the commander of British troops in southern England, had feared with good cause that if the Germans ever landed then Britain was finished. Not everyone agrees with that doom-laden conclusion, but, thanks to winning the Battle of Britain in the skies, the RAF had rendered that question moot. No German invasion was now possible and Britain, under Churchill breathed to live another day.

But there was something far more important that Churchill knew, and far too few British people understood. Being half-American himself (through his mother) he knew that only from the USA could effective rescue come. Only the USA could actually defeat Hitler. We now take American power for granted but Churchill was in a very small minority in Britain at the time when he did so as well.

And for the USA to be able to help to defeat Hitler, they needed the geographical equivalent of a landing base from which to do so. That base was the United Kingdom, just off the coast of Continental Europe. D-Day and 1944 were still a long way off and in September 1940 the USA was still neutral.

But now that Britain had survived and had actually defeated the supposedly invincible Germans, those Americans, such as Roosevelt, who loved freedom and democracy now had the excuse that they wanted to come to Britain's aid, albeit, as Roosevelt put it, 'short of war itself'. The USA, the 'arsenal of democracy' would now be able to implement plans such as Lend-Lease to provide Britain with the weapons without which survival would be impossible. In a free and fighting United Kingdom, the USA would have its future base ready for the time when they could enter the war. That was still fifteen months away when Sealion was postponed, but it was now possible to start planning.

The 'few' – all 2,917 of them – of the RAF really had turned the tide.

OPERATION COMPASS

December 9th 1940–February 9th 1941

One of the great myths of World War II is that the British never had a victory before their iconic triumph at Alamein in November 1942, when General Bernard Montgomery, later Field Marshal Viscount Montgomery *of Alamein*, beat the famous German 'Desert Fox', Field Marshal Erwin Rommel.

But this is in fact entirely untrue. British (and British Empire troops from India, Australia and New Zealand) were vanquishing their Axis enemy, December 1940–February 1941, in a series of victorious battles all across North Africa. For 494 British and Empire losses there were not just 3,000 Italians killed but also 115,000 taken prisoner and 400 of the enemy's tanks destroyed. The forces, under the command of General Sir Richard O'Connor – the Western Desert Force, which included the famous 7th Armoured Division, the 'Desert Rats' – managed to advance some 500 miles in December–February, almost wiping out the numerically superior Italian forces in three months of continuous success.

By any standard, this is military victory on a heroic scale. But it remains almost unknown in Britain or Australia, and Sir Richard O'Connor is as unfamiliar a name as that of Montgomery is illustrious. How was this and what were Britain and Italy doing fighting one another in North Africa, a long way from Europe?

The British Empire in India, the 'Raj', was the 'Jewel in the Crown' of Britain's imperial possessions. After the Suez Canal opened in the nineteenth century, that waterway became, via the Mediterranean, the most vital conduit from Britain itself to India and other British possessions beyond (such as Singapore and Malaya). To guard this route had been essential to the United Kingdom's most critical defence interests for decades, and Britain had occupied Egypt 1882–1922, effectively ruling the country. Now in 1940 Egypt was notionally independent, but there was still a large British army present. And with the discovery of oil in the Middle East in the early twentieth century, from which so much of Britain's crucial oil supplies came, the defence of the region became more important than ever. If the Axis conquered Egypt, then not only would the Suez Canal fall into enemy hands but so too might the vast oil wealth of the Middle East. (At this time Britain also controlled Palestine and what are now Jordan and Iraq.)

Italy had ruled Libya since 1912, and in June 1940 Mussolini had opportunistically joined his Axis partner Hitler in the war. As a result by late 1940 the Italian dictator ordered his troops to attack the British in Egypt.

After Dunkirk British forces had been expelled from European soil. But very bravely, especially in the light of a potential German invasion, Churchill decided to reinforce the British (and Empire) armies in Egypt, ready to take on the Axis whenever and wherever possible.

So when the Italians began their campaign, British-led troops in the region (under the overall command of General Sir Archibald Wavell) were ready for them, moving seventy miles from their main base in order to confront the Italian invaders. Operation Compass, to use its British codename, had now begun.

Disaster began almost straight away for the Italian forces, under supreme command of Marshal Graziani. At the Battle for the Camps the Italians were routed and the Italian leader, General Maletti, lost his life.

Soon British and Empire forces were streaming over the border into Libya. On December 10th–11th a British and Indian force overwhelmed the Italians at the Battle of Sidi Barrani and a defeat now turned into a rout. By January 22nd 1941 British and Australian forces had captured the key Libyan port of Tobruk. (This city was to prove symbolic of whoever was winning in North Africa – it was to fall later to the Germans and then had to be recaptured by the British over the course of 1941–1943.) This successful siege came, however, at the loss of 100 Australian lives, one-third of all those involved in Operation Compass. On February 7th the Western Desert Force crushed the Italians at the Battle of Beda Fomm, and by the time that the victorious British and Empire forces stopped at El Agheila on February 9th 1941, O'Connor was able to declare not just a halt but complete victory. As we saw at the start, his troops had gone almost 500 miles with very few casualties and captured thousands of enemy troops and equipment.

So what happened?

The answer is that controversial decisions taken hundreds of miles away in London and Athens completely derailed O'Connor's achievements.

On October 28th 1940 Italian troops invaded Greece (Italy having ruled Albania since 1939.) This proved an equal disaster for Mussolini as the events in North Africa – and to add to this, by January 1941 the British-led successful liberation of Ethiopia from Italian rule was well under way.

Churchill sent Anthony Eden, the Foreign Secretary, and the Chief of the Imperial General Staff, Field Marshal Sir John Dill, to investigate whether or not Britain ought to aid the Greeks. Sir Archibald Wavell, whose command area included Greece, was also consulted. Eden and Dill warmly recommended that Britain had to be honourable and send military help to Greece. But the problem was that the only spare troops were those in the Middle East, including many of the triumphant forces under O'Connor. Aid to Greece would mean denuding O'Connor of thousands of his soldiers just at Britain's very moment of victory. It was not an easy decision for the authorities in London to make.

Churchill swayed one way and then the other, and in the end took the decision to aid Greece. Thousands of O'Connor's troops were sent from North Africa to the Greek mainland to, as we shall now see, utter disaster.

Many historians – such as John Keegan and Evan Mawdsley – now think that this was one of Churchill's biggest strategic blunders of the war. It effectively seized defeat from the jaws of victory. Many soldiers at the time, including Montgomery's future Chief of Staff Freddy de Guingand, were also appalled. But helping Greece seemed the honourable thing to do, and Churchill made his decision on the basis of foreign policy and moral rectitude not strategy

O'Connor was rested by Wavell, and his successor in the Western Desert, General Sir Philip Neame, was nowhere near as effective a commander. This was now disastrous, since on February 6th Hitler had ordered one of the best German generals, Erwin Rommel, to command a newly formed *Afrika Korps* with key Panzer divisions, to help the beleaguered Italians keep from losing the war. On March 24th 1941 Rommel began his offensive, and O'Connor (and Neame) had the bad luck to be captured on April 6th by a German patrol. Soon the Germans would be blasting the now heavily reduced British forces all the way back to Egypt. O'Connor's victory roll was over and so, until he managed to escape some years later, was his military career. Britain had won a major battle but it had, for all sorts of reasons, good and bad, thrown it away.

However, the well-known historian Sir Ian Kershaw has pointed out one silver lining. Britain lost Compass because of Greece. But, as he says, Mussolini sent tens of thousands of Italian troops to Greece whom he could otherwise have sent to North Africa, to join Graziani's forces there. Had that been the case, the odds against Britain would have been far higher – and not even O'Connor would have won. If that is true, we lost – but in a place, in North Africa, where we could hang on and by sheer dogged persistence survive to fight another day, which was sadly not the British experience in Crete, as we shall see . . .

THE BATTLE OF CAPE MATAPAN

March 27th–29th 1941

When we think of World War II we usually recall the epic naval battles fought in the Pacific, or the Atlantic and Arctic convoys bringing vital supplies from the USA over to Britain or to the USSR.

But one of the key naval battles was fought by the Royal Navy (with help from Australian ships) in the Mediterranean, near the Peloponnese peninsula of Greece in late March 1941.

Ships under Admiral Sir Andrew Cunningham were able to intercept a large number of Italian warships near Greek waters. The discovery of these enemy vessels was very much thanks to decrypts from Bletchley Park, who had successfully broken the Italian naval codes. This victory was also critical because it then enabled the Royal Navy to evacuate thousands of British and

Empire soldiers first from Greece and then from Crete, which would have been impossible if the Italians had been able to achieve naval superiority in the Eastern Mediterranean.

The battle effectively ended the Italian ability to threaten the British in that part of the Mediterranean, a rare piece of good news for Britain at a time when everything else (such as in Greece and later North Africa) seemed to be going wrong.

THE FALL OF CRETE

May 20th–June 1st 1941

The capture of mainland Greece by the Germans in April 1941, along with the successful seizure of Crete the following month, was one of the biggest British disasters of the war. While not many British and Empire (mainly Australian) troops were killed, some 17,000 of them were captured by the Germans in the island of Crete – on top of the nearly 14,000 already taken prisoners in the fall of Greece a few weeks earlier. As Sir John Keegan rightly pointed out, this was a second Dunkirk. But it was the Allies who learnt the lessons of failure and the Germans who forgot those of their success.

The Italian invasion of Greece had been such a fiasco that Hitler decided that the only thing to do was to send a major German expeditionary force to the Balkans to sort out the mess.

He had contemplated war against Greece late in 1940 but now the time had come. The invasion was codenamed Marita, and it enabled Hitler to achieve several goals at once. He had Bulgaria and Romania under his effective control already as junior allies of the Axis. He thought Yugoslavia was as well. But in a brilliant coup with British aid, brave Yugoslav army officers overthrew the Prince Regent, and installed a pro-Allied regime. Hitler was furious – the Yugoslavs would have to be punished.

So Marita, a mainly German assault on the Balkans, was launched on April 6th. German troops invaded Yugoslavia directly, conquering the country in just eleven days. They invaded Greece via their ally Bulgaria, crushing both the Greeks and the British and Empire forces by the end of the month. It was, as we saw, partly a result of Churchill's quixotic but strategically flawed idea of helping the Greeks, with thousands of British, Australian and other troops now Nazi prisoners of war.

Many British and Empire troops did manage to make it to Crete, where there was an army commanded by General Bernard Freyberg, a New Zealander and holder of the Victoria Cross (VC) for bravery from World War I.

The German invasion of Crete shows two things. First men who are highly intrepid individuals, such as Freyberg, do not necessarily make the wisest commanders. (The same was true, for example, of General Gort, also a VC but a failure in 1940 in charge of the British Expeditionary Force or BEF.) Second, the existence of ULTRA, the Allied ability to break German codes through the Enigma machines at Bletchley Park, does not lead to victory if the user fails to understand what he is being told.

There is no doubting the immense courage not just of Freyberg himself but also that of the British and Empire (New Zealand forces on Crete) army there to defend the island. Malta survived far worse odds than Crete yet survived the war albeit battered but ultimately unconquered. The ULTRA decrypts made it clear to Freyberg that the Germans were coming by parachute and that the key airfields, especially Maleme, had to be defended. But Freyberg instead prepared his key troops to defend the beaches, which he thought would be the German target, and this despite ULTRA and the fact that the Royal Navy were preventing any such seaborne invasion by the Germans from taking place.

The New Zealander and British forces fought gallantly to defend the island, including the airfields, which soon became the real centre of the battle when German parachutists started landing there in huge numbers.

But in the end, the odds were overwhelming and the dispersal of British and Empire soldiers, many of whom were initially in the wrong place, meant that the Germans, once they had landed, soon had the upper hand.

After just ten days the Allies had to cease fighting, surrendering formally on June 1st. Thankfully the Royal Navy were able to evacuate many of the beleaguered forces, one of whom, the writer Evelyn Waugh, would satirise the events in his *Sword of Honour* wartime trilogy of novels. But thousands more soldiers were stranded and taken prisoner by the Germans, with all their equipment also falling into Axis hands. Disaster in Greece was now followed by another in Crete, just as Rommel was beginning to do his worst to the British and Empire forces in North Africa. Things were not looking good.

One myth, propagated both by Hitler and by Churchill, both

of whom believed it to be true: Marita caused a fatal delay to the truly epic German campaign not just of 1941 but of the whole war – Barbarossa, the invasion of the USSR in June 1941.

They both believed that the few weeks' delay of Barbarossa was caused by Marita, and that had Hitler not needed to invade and conquer Yugoslavia and Greece but could have launched Barbarossa earlier and thus conquered Moscow and won the Second World War.

But as Sir Ian Kershaw and many others have argued, this is not true. As we shall see, most experts now think that Germany could never had conquered the USSR whatever month Barbarossa was launched, since the entire enterprise was a pipe dream from the beginning. Weather conditions also delayed the beginning, so that even if Marita had never happened, a pre-June start for Barbarossa was utterly impracticable. Hitler made a monumental error in attacking the USSR from which he would never recover. Churchill erred in his desire to help the Greeks, but soon events would turn in his favour, as 1941 would unfold.

PART TWO: II

1941–1942

Early War: The Eastern Front

BARBAROSSA:
THE GERMAN INVASION OF THE USSR

June 22nd 1941

June 22nd 1941 is the day that the war changed. No longer could Germany win the conflict.

This may seem a strange way to introduce the German invasion of the USSR – Operation Barbarossa. For the first few weeks the invaders were triumphant. Over four million Red Army troops died and hundreds of thousands of their forces were captured, with eventually three million Soviet prisoners dying in German captivity. The Wehrmacht almost reached as far as Moscow itself, with some of the front-line troops actually able to see the Kremlin.

Yet the Germans did not win. And this, a new breed of historians is arguing, is exactly the point. Not merely did they fail to capture Moscow, but they went on to military catastrophe, with no fewer than eighty-five per cent of World War II German casualties being on the Eastern Front, in the war with the USSR. The vast expanses of Soviet territory were just simply far too much. The Germans, who thought that they had won within the first week or so, were doomed from the very beginning.

Let us just get an idea of the sheer vastness of the scale of what the Germans needed to do, in comparison with their earlier, far easier, West European victories. As Evan Mawdsley, a leading expert on the USSR under Stalin reminds us: 'The breadth of the active front in France and the Low Countries [in 1940] was 150 miles; the breadth of the main front in Russia was 750 miles.' The key German victory capturing the Somme-Aisne Line to the French capital Paris was seventy-five miles long. From the Dvina-Dnieper Line in Russia to Moscow was 350 miles – and that itself was a vast 350 miles from the German start line on June 22nd, so 700 miles from the first day of Barbarossa to the Russian capital, Moscow.

Then as General Halder, Hitler's Chief of the Army General Staff, discovered to his horror: 'At the start of the war we had counted on about 200 enemy divisions. We have now counted 360 . . . And if we knock out a dozen of them, then the Russian puts up another dozen . . .'

Indeed as the writer Philip Bell sums it up: 'By his attack on the Soviet Union, Hitler brought ultimate destruction upon himself and upon his country.'

Hitler had issued instructions to start preparing for war as far back as July 3rd 1940, when planning began. The order to create Barbarossa, Führer Directive No. 21 was created on December 18th 1940. In this document, Hitler decreed that: 'The German

Armed Forces must be prepared to crush Soviet Russia in a quick campaign even before the end of the war against England.' Hitler was, in other words, deliberately launching a two-front war, fighting Britain in the West and the USSR in the East.

One important point – the German invasion of the USSR was pre-planned. For a brief while in the 1990s there was a debate launched by a Russian writer under the pseudonym 'Suvarov' that Stalin had originally been planning to strike first. This theory, while interesting, has been demolished by the Israeli writer Gabriel Gorodetsky and by the British historian Sir Ian Kershaw. Soviet military doctrine was certainly based upon 'offensive' thinking, and Stalin had made such a speech, praising such a strategy, in May 1941. But Stalin knew that as a result of his own purges in 1937–1938, in which tens of thousands of Red Army senior officers were murdered (including some of the very senior commanders), that his army would be nowhere near ready enough for actual offensive action until at least well into 1942. June 1941, when Barbarossa began, was thus a hideous shock to Stalin and to the entire Soviet leadership, as we shall soon see.

The vastness of the German campaign, which has rightly been called by many one of the biggest operations in the history of warfare, can be seen in the size of the invasion force. There were 3,100,000 German troops along with at least 650,000 allies – mostly from Finland and Romania, but also in due time from Italy and Spain as well. There were 4,000 tanks – and, incredible though this seems when we are thinking of twentieth-century warfare – no fewer than 750,000 horses.

(A note here – different books give very divergent statistics when it comes to the Second World War. Another book gives just

625,000 horses, rather fewer than above. Either way there were a *lot* of horses! And horses need gigantic amounts of fodder and upkeep, as many of them were transport animals and not cavalry mounts. In addition, horses suffer as much from great heat and extreme cold as do humans, as the German would soon discover . . .)

Stalin, knowing that the USSR was not ready for war, had been doing all possible not to provoke Hitler into an attack. This is perhaps the most persuasive argument for one of the biggest mysteries of the war. Everyone was telling Stalin that a gigantic German army was amassing on the Soviet border (which, remember, included Eastern Poland, far further to the West than before September 1939).

His key spies, such as Richard Sorge, an NKVD spy in the German Embassy in Tokyo, could not have been more explicit. The famous 'Lucy Ring' of Soviet spies in Switzerland told him the same. The British, who had uncovered many German plans from the ULTRA decrypts, warned him as strongly as possible. Any spotter plane could detect the enormous German troop movements, which could have only one possible purpose. Yet Stalin ignored all of this completely! The only reason why he did so would be that he was so aware of the hideous deficiencies of the Red Army. Therefore he did all possible to appease Hitler in what turned out to be the entirely vain hope that war would come at a moment convenient to Stalin and not to Hitler. The launch of Barbarossa at 4.15 am on the June 22nd destroyed all those illusions.

Within just a few days, the Red Army Air Force had virtually ceased to exist, as thousands of planes were destroyed upon the ground. Three entire Soviet field armies were simply wiped out, their soldiers either killed or taken prisoner. In the battle for Smolensk alone some 750,000 Red Army troops were captured and by September over two million Soviet soldiers were dead.

Churchill had, after the Russian Revolution of 1917, been vehemently anti-Bolshevik. But now he put ideology aside – Britain and the USSR were allies and, despite many ups and downs and misunderstandings, were to remain so for the rest of the war. Limited British supplies began their perilous journey to the Soviet Union. Once the USA was in the conflict, they also sent vast amounts of material, much of it via Vladivostok in the east.

Few, however, expected the Russians to survive for long, perhaps for a while not even Stalin himself who, towards the end of June, had what one could describe as a brief nervous breakdown, before pulling himself together and taking charge.

For the Allies, watching the Germans seize territory of hundreds of thousands of square miles of Soviet territory, the outcome of the war did not look good.

THE FIRST BATTLE OF KIEV

July 7th or August 23rd 1941–September 19th 1941

This is the only battle in this book for which there are two start dates. The earlier one represents the Soviet perspective, the latter (perhaps more accurately) that of the invading German army.

Whole books have been written about this single epic encounter between Red Army and Wehrmacht troops. It has been described, surely without exaggeration, as possibly Hitler's greatest single victory of the war. German forces took Kiev, destroyed an entire Soviet army group, and captured 665,000 prisoners. Other writers have described it as the most successful encirclement ever and certainly, as American writer Mitchell Bard puts it, 'the largest mass capture in military history', with a mere 15,000 Red Army troops able to escape. The Wehrmacht was able completely to surround a Soviet army and wipe it out. General

Mikhail Kirponos, the Red Army commander, lost his life in the action. Whatever way one describes it, the First Battle of Kiev (the second one being fought in radically different circumstances in 1943) was a massive victory for Hitler and his forces.

However, things were not that simple . . .

First, by now the Germans had lost 185,000 troops in a mere three months – this was far more than the 102,000 they had lost in the whole of the rest of the war up until then, the invasion of France and of the Balkans and the battles in North Africa all combined. They had also, by now, lost more Luftwaffe planes than in the entire Battle of Britain back in 1940.

Hitler and his generals now began to argue with each other about what to do next. Remember that the whole concept of Barbarossa depended on being able to carry out a *blitzkrieg* in the USSR of the kind that had proved so wonderfully successful in the rest of Europe up until now. And, as we have seen, the sheer enormity of the Soviet Union meant that while the Russians had lost millions of men captured or killed, and entire armies, they were still there and still fighting in seemingly irreplaceable numbers.

For what he decided, even before Kiev, was to split the main assault into different directions.

One part, Army Group North, was to go towards the area including Leningrad, now called St Petersburg, the former Russian imperial capital. Despite the loss of over a million civilians from starvation, Leningrad was miraculously to hold out throughout the entire war unconquered, while the Germans were able to conquer the Baltic States easily, including Riga, later notorious for the horrors of its Jewish ghetto.

Hitler was very aware that the Ukraine was the breadbasket of Russia. One of the major problems that Germany had faced in 1918 was that the Allies were, in effect, able to starve the Germans into submission and into signing the Treaty of Versailles. To capture the Ukraine and its agricultural resources for the German Reich had been one of Hitler's goals since he wrote *Mein Kampf* and now he ordered his generals in the two other fronts to divide. Army Group Centre was therefore to consolidate and Army Group South was to capture as much of the Ukraine as possible.

Some of the German generals simply wanted to go straight on to Moscow. After the war, when interrogated by the victorious Allies, they protested that Hitler, a mere former army corporal, had insisted upon a strategy that threw inevitable victory away and created a strategic situation in which the Germans could no longer win.

But it is debatable whether a direct assault on Moscow would have been successful, whatever the generals argued. On October 7th the *rasputitsa* season began – interestingly the earliest it had been since 1812 and Napoleon's equally unsuccessful attempt to beat the Russians that year. This form of weather is a uniquely Russian form of slush or quagmire that turns the roads into mud and transportation all but impossible.

It is because of this that people often call 'General Winter' the greatest ever Russian commander, as the treacherous conditions of winter make normal advances impossible for those – like the Germans – completely unprepared for such extreme weather conditions. And much of this, as the events showed, turned out to be true.

But new thinking argues that it was more than just the

quagmires, as profoundly unhelpful to German equipment and soldiers as they were. The German *blitzkrieg* successes had been mainly on proper roads, and in the ever-increasing spaces of Russia, the primitive nature of the roads, and the fact that the railways were on a different gauge system from the whole of the rest of Europe, meant that hundreds of German tanks and trucks simply broke down in ways that could not easily be prepared.

The very success of the Wehrmacht in covering hundreds of miles in just a few weeks had put them too far away from their supply bases back in Germany – they had massively overextended. The Russians, however, had constant replacement capabilities, not just in terms of equipment, but also in terms above all of manpower. There were simply millions more Soviet citizens than German. Therefore, while German troops who died could not be replaced there was a gigantic reservoir of manpower of replacement troops ready for the USSR, how ever many millions of forces they lost to the invaders.

So the slush and the onset of sub-zero temperatures created a massive disaster for the Germans: the lack of winter clothing for the Wehrmacht has become a legendary cause of the failure to capture Moscow in 1941. But the new thinking, that the Soviet army ability not just to have troops in warm clothes, but millions of fresh soldiers to replace those who had died, as a critical factor in Red Army success has not until recently been taken seriously enough. In addition, countless German pieces of equipment had been irrevocably damaged in the *warm* weather of July–September. Hitler's decision in July to split the attack may have annoyed his generals, but it made no difference to the outcome of the war itself.

Then in September Hitler decided, after the huge successes in the Ukraine, that the time had come to go for Moscow after all. On September 16th the head of Army Group Centre, General von Bock, announced Operation Typhoon, the assault upon the Soviet capital. On October 1st the attack began.

OPERATION TYPHOON AND THE BATTLE FOR MOSCOW

October 1st 1941–January 5th 1942

The Battle for Moscow, called by the Germans Operation Typhoon, was, one could argue, one of the two turning points of the whole Second World War. The other one, which also took place around the same time, was America's entry into the conflict. The first event meant that Hitler could no longer win, and the second made Allied victory inevitable. So the period we are looking at now is the pivotal point of World War II.

On October 1st 1941 the Germans unleashed no fewer than two million men (including three Panzer groups), with the hope of being shortly in the streets of Moscow. By October 13th they had reached Borodino, the site of Napoleon's pyrrhic victory over the Russians in 1812. Things looked more and more like an effortless German victory.

But on October 5th Stalin had already made the key decision to set up a new line of defence: the Mozhaisk Line, roughly seventy-five miles west of Moscow. Also created at that time was a new 'strategic echelon' along the Volga River, with no fewer than nine reserve armies ready for the fight.

Logistics are often overlooked – the dash of battle, the concept of thousands of tanks engaged in battle, the smell of cordite and tales of courage: these are the things of which stories are made. But in fact logistics are at the heart of victory. Now this would prove true for Moscow, and thus for the fate of the war.

In September 1940 Japan had signed the Axis Agreement with Italy and with Germany – hence the name given to them during the war of the 'Axis Powers'. But in reality there was very little co-ordination between these three countries, especially as events would prove to their disadvantage and eventual ruin. Japan had not known of the Molotov–Ribbentrop Pact in August 1939 and had been furious with Germany as a result, as we saw. Now instead they would plan, fatefully, to attack south towards the European possessions in South East Asia, instead of north against the USSR via Siberia. Their disastrous loss at Khalkhin-Gol had convinced many key decision-makers of the former option over the latter. A two-front war, against the USSR and the USA, was to them inconceivable. So in April 1941 Japan signed a non-aggression pact with the Soviet Union.

The importance of this little-known treaty cannot be exaggerated – it could be said to have altered the entire course of the war. Stalin was to break the pact, but only after May 1945, after VE-Day: he too knew the stupidity of fighting on two fronts. (As we shall see, the USA was able to do this easily, fighting in the Pacific and in Europe, but that is for now another story . . .)

This meant that as the Germans seemed at the very gates of Moscow, Stalin was able to move vast armies from the Soviet Far East to the defence of European Russia and the capital in particular. One of the most important German errors of the war – one could say an utterly fatal one in the long term – was that they consistently and massively underestimated the sheer size of the Red Army. And as we saw, even in the victory days of the summer of 1941, the fact that Soviet troops could be slaughtered and captured in their millions (two million and more by September 1941) but effortlessly replaced by new and fresh armies made the absolute critical difference. The Red Army had millions of potential soldiers in reserve. One estimate has no fewer than 1.177 million Red Army troops in the Eastern USSR district in September 1941. With war with Japan now unlikely, these troops could all be used for the defence of Moscow. But by December 1941 the Wehrmacht was already nearing the casualty rate that made replacements from the Reich impossible.

So even though German forces actually reached the Mozhaisk Line by October 10th, all was not lost for the Soviets.

Stalin did not realise this immediately. On October 15th he panicked briefly, ordering the relocation of the entire Soviet government and defence apparatus to the town of Kuibyshev (now called Samara), some 650 miles distant on the Volga River. For two days, October 16th–18th, there was utter panic in Moscow.

However, on October 18th Stalin made one of his most important decisions of the war – he announced that he would stay in Moscow. Retreat to Kuibyshev was not for him. This had a colossal impact on morale. The NKVD, the dreaded secret police, now made doubly sure that cowards would be shot and Moscow defended to the bitter end. The annual commemoration of the Bolshevik Revolution was held – as usual – on November 7th. More important still were the 831,000 Red Army troops transferred from Siberia. By the time that the Germans were almost in the suburbs of Moscow no fewer than ninety-nine new divisions were ready for the fight.

It is frequently said that the unusual cold – as noted the coldest Russian winter since Napoleon's failure in 1812 – was the key cause of the German failure. But new thinking, while taking into account the weather and the utter lack of preparation for it by the Germans, has a different perspective that is wholly convincing. As retired Glasgow academic Ewan Mawdsley has stated: 'The Germans did not fail to get to Moscow because the weather broke; they were caught by the freeze because they had failed to reach Moscow.' Several factors made a difference in the ability to defend Moscow: the extra ninety-nine Red Army divisions, Stalin's decision to stay in Moscow and his recall of his most successful commander, General Zhukov, back to lead the fight for the capital.

With Zhukov – and the sinister NKVD security chief Lavrentiy Beria – in charge, some 250,000 Muscovite civilians started to dig anti-tank trenches. Bridges were mined and hundreds of villages were torched in a scorched-earth policy to do all possible to fight to the last man, woman and child to defend Moscow.

Just at this moment Hitler took an extraordinary decision. Rommel needed aircraft against the British in North Africa.

Compared to the titanic struggle in central Russia, the war there was a minnow. But Hitler ordered the Luftwaffe to send reinforcements to Rommel all the same, thereby denuding the Wehrmacht as they stood only miles away from the gates of Moscow.

The attack seemed to be going well, especially that part of it led by Panzer General Heinz Guderian's Second Panzer Army, who created a large salient around 170 miles south of Moscow, reaching a long way until halted by heavy Red Army resistance at Tula.

Soon the vanguard of the German forces was just twenty-one miles from Moscow itself.

But now came the Red Army counter-attack of the new armies that the Germans did not think existed. Between December 5th–6th 1941 the Soviet counter-offensive began, and it would be the ruin of Hitler's dreams.

How much difference would it have made if the Germans *had* captured Moscow? The psychological impact would have been colossal. But success did no good to Napoleon and one suspects Hitler would have found the same. The Soviet Union was simply too vast. Therefore the German notion of conquering European Russia when they launched Barbarossa in June 1941 was surely a chimera? The new academic thesis that the entire operation was doomed from the beginning thus applies to Moscow – capturing it would have made but a fleeting difference, and made none at all to the inevitability of German defeat.

THE BATTLE OF VIAZ'MA-BRIANSK

October 2nd–7th 1941

The encirclement, annihilation and utter defeat of four entire Soviet armies between the towns of Viaz'ma and Briansk is perhaps the most famous military engagement of which most of us have never heard. It is a battle of extraordinary import, yet has no entry of its own on Wikipedia. And one historian, the specialist on Soviet history Ewan Mawdsley, in his book *Thunder in the East* described it as 'one of the greatest successes of German arms in the entire Second World War. It was perhaps, too, the most ignominious defeat suffered by the Soviets.' Over 760,000 Red Army troops were taken prisoner, five top Soviet generals were killed (Petrov and Rakutin) or captured, and since one million of the original 1.25 million of the Red Army troops were lost, some 240,000 or more must have been killed in the German onslaught. So great was the Soviet defeat that it was hushed up until recently.

This is a disaster on a major scale – some seventy Red Army divisions had vanished – and to Hitler's joy the way to Moscow now seemed to be wide open. Victory could not be far away.

So why have we never heard of so large an encounter? Why would a key German victory, like the one we have just seen, be ignored or even hushed up? It does not quite fit into the pattern of early German victories and the epic Soviet turnaround on December 5th in Moscow.

The answer is surely what happened next – the German failure to capture Moscow. The encirclement of Kiev, and the total disintegration of Red Army units on the frontier with Germany when the invasion began has long been public information.

But the Battle of Viaz'ma-Briansk was a key battle all the same. On October 8th, the day after the defeat, Stalin recalled to Moscow General Georgi Zhukov, who had been briefly serving on the Leningrad front. As we saw in the latter's great victory over the Japanese at Khalkhin-Gol in 1939, Zhukov was destined for greater things, and now he was in charge of the defence of Moscow itself. Stalin had learnt the right lesson from the crisis and soon the seemingly unstoppable German juggernaut would finally be coming to a halt.

OPERATION CRUSADER

November 18th–December 30th 1941

Rommel was 'the Desert Fox', a foe against whom British, Indian, Australian, New Zealand and, after 1942, also American forces would fight in the wastelands of the North African Desert until 1943. After D-Day in 1944 they would fight him again in France.

He was, however, not invincible and the frustration in studying Operation Crusader is how close the British and Empire troops came to beating him long before the heroic Bernard Montgomery arrived in 1942 and famously vanquished him at the Battle of Alamein in November of that memorable year.

Rommel's *Afrika Korps* forces landed in Tripoli (in Libya) in February 1941 and by April they had already taken back much of the territory so valiantly won by O'Connor in Compass.

Unfortunately for the Germans, they failed to capture the key town of Tobruk, still in Allied hands since January. This inevitably slowed up what had seemed like Rommel's inexorable progress back to Egypt.

Wavell therefore decided to launch a counter-strike, urged on by Churchill, who had been able to obtain for the British a large number of American tanks thanks to the Lend-Lease programme authorised by the US Congress that March.

But Battleaxe in June 1941 was a complete fiasco, with the British singularly failing to dislodge or repel the German-led forces. (There were still Italians in North Africa, but now under Rommel's overall command in charge of Axis armies.) This ended Wavell's career in North Africa, as Churchill did not tolerate failure. Wavell swapped posts with General Sir Claude Auchinleck, the veteran Commander-in-Chief of British forces in India.

While all this was happening in North Africa, the Allies had great success in another part of the Middle East. In June–July 1941 British and Empire forces, along with Free French troops, were able to dislodge Vichy French loyalists who had been in command of Syria and Lebanon since France's surrender in 1940. While less known than the battles in the Western desert, this achievement was crucial since it protected vital Allied oil interests in the Middle East.

By November Auchinleck felt that his armies – now including the newly formed British 8th Army – were ready for counter-attack. Crusader was launched and, by the end of 1941, the British and Empire forces had almost driven the Germans and Italians back to the lines that O'Connor had reached in February. As historian Evan Mawdsley has rightly commented, the offensive was 'the first victory of the British Army against German ground forces'.

December 1941 also saw the entry of the USA into the war. But at the same time the Japanese invasion of British imperial possessions in South East Asia had also begun, and thus posed a threat to Australia itself, in the region known by its geographical designation, the Near North. Unfortunately for Australia, Allied resources were now needed elsewhere. And Hitler chose this time to transfer more than twenty U-boats to the Mediterranean, to do all possible to prevent supplies reaching Auchinleck's forces. Without key supplies, it would be hard to pursue Rommel further, as the British were soon to find out . . .

THE FIRST BATTLE OF ROSTOV

November 21st–December 1st 1941

With all the epic battles taking place on a gigantic scale in Central Russia in 1941, we tend to forget that one of Hitler's key ideas was to send a large army south with the eventual goal of capturing the oil fields of the Caucasus, which, if Baku had been taken, would have supplied the Wehrmacht with enough petrol for years.

The Germans got a long way eventually, but never quite made it to Baku or Maikop. One of the reasons for this was a rare Soviet victory in 1941, at the key town of Rostov-on-Don, a city on the river just up from the Sea of Azov.

In the earlier battle for the Sea of Azov itself, Army Group South was under the command of Field Marshal Gerd von Rundstedt, the highly acclaimed conqueror of both Poland and

France. In their September–October battles the German run of success continued, with well over 100,000 Red Army troops taken prisoner, more than 200 tanks captured and numerous artillery pieces as well.

On November 21st German Panzer troops, under the command of Sepp Dietrich and the elite *Leibstandarte SS Adolf Hitler* captured Rostov. With Dietrich's close links to Hitler going back to early Nazi days, this was a source of personal pride for Hitler.

But the Germans had, as in Central Russia, managed to overextend themselves. The Red Army was able to launch a counter-attack. Rundstedt, thinking strategically, realised that the German army was overstretched and so should execute a strategic withdrawal to a more easily defended base. Hitler was furious and immediately sacked Rundstedt, despite the latter's huge eminence and experience. But when the Führer flew from his Wolf's Lair headquarters in East Prussia to the front-line headquarters at Mariupul, even he was forced to allow for a withdrawal. The Red Army was able to recapture the city, to great rejoicing all the way to Stalin in the Kremlin.

The Germans were no longer invincible. Rostov would fall to them eventually in 1942, but the juggernaut of Barbarossa was now finally beginning to come off its wheels.

PART TWO: III

1941–1942

The USA Enters the War

THE GREER INCIDENT

September 4th 1941

One of the greatest difficulties faced by President Roosevelt before Japan attacked the USA at Pearl Harbor in December 1941 was how best to help the British, short of war. Roosevelt himself, like many generous Americans, very much wanted the British not only to survive but also to win against the evils of Nazi Germany. But isolationism – the powerful sentiment that the US should stay completely out of all foreign entanglements – was still a very powerful factor in American politics. As late as the Presidential election of November 1940 Roosevelt felt obliged to promise the US electorate that he would keep their sons out of war overseas. Nor was it a partisan issue as there were zealous Democrat isolationists in places such as the US Senate, whom Roosevelt could not ignore, and Republicans in his Administration who by contrast actively wanted the USA to go to war both to defend Britain against Germany and also to prevent Japanese expansionism in the Pacific.

On March 11th 1941 Roosevelt persuaded Congress (the American equivalent of Parliament) to agree to Lend-Lease, a US programme that theoretically lent crucial military supplies to friendly nations, which would be critical to the survival of those countries against enemy attacks. Britain would be by far the main beneficiary of this scheme, in their struggle against Germany, but China also benefitted in their long-haul fight against the Japanese invaders. In theory the draconian US Neutrality Acts passed by Congress in the even more isolationist 1930s were still in play, but Lend-Lease enabled Roosevelt legally to subvert that legislation by helping give supplies to those who needed them while preserving the fig leaf of theoretical US neutrality.

Then in August 1941 Roosevelt went on what people were told was a 'fishing trip'. In reality it was nothing of the kind. He travelled to Canadian waters, to Placentia Bay, where he met with Winston Churchill who had crossed the Atlantic to meet him. The meetings began on August 9th and on August 14th Churchill and Roosevelt together issued the Atlantic Charter, a powerful declaration of common aims and a passionate defence of democratic values and ideals. The USA was still technically neutral, but by now it was apparent where American loyalties and friendship lay so far as the leadership were concerned.

Supplies to Britain needed American ships in which to carry them. Strictly speaking such vessels were neutral boats, and should have been immune to German U-boat attacks. But in practice they were carrying vitally needed war materials to the

United Kingdom, and therefore the German navy regarded them as *de facto* enemy ships, and treated them accordingly.

On September 4th 1941 the USS *Greer* came under attack and fired back. This was entirely understandable in the circumstances, except that in legal theory the USA was not at war with Germany. In retrospect it is astonishing that this did not provoke actual war, but the outward pretence was still maintained even though a war of words between the USA and the Third Reich now ensued.

People have been astonished that Hitler took the initiative in December 1941 – after the Japanese attack on Pearl Harbor – to declare war on the USA in solidarity with his ally Japan. But incidents such as the USS *Greer* show that war had been simmering between the USA and the Third Reich for some time, and Hitler had long since regarded the US as a German enemy. By the time of the incident, global war was surely inevitable, and just around the corner.

PEARL HARBOR

December 7th 1941

Pearl Harbor was, as President Roosevelt told the American public, a day which would live in infamy. It is one of the best-known dates in history, the date upon which the Japanese attacked the US Naval Base in Pearl Harbor in Hawaii.

It is also the day, as Churchill realised, that turned the tide of the entire war – he went to sleep that night knowing that the war was now won and that Britain was safe. He was proved right of course, but we should not forget that the reason why Churchill's dreams of American aid came true was not because of the Japanese attack itself, but because, in solidarity with Japan, Hitler declared war on the USA. It is the second event, which, from Britain's point of view, is the more important, since in theory the USA could have been at war with Japan only and not with Germany.

And in such an eventuality, American aid to Britain would have been very late if it had come at all.

One can also say that the attack was the day upon which the USA became the world superpower that it has been ever since. From the start of Warren Harding's unfortunate Presidency in 1921–1923 the predominant mood in the USA had been isolationism, a desire to keep as far out of the world's affairs as possible. The USA was unquestionably the number-one global power in economic terms, but until the 1940s it had an army the same size as that of Belgium. Because it was the Japanese that took the war to the USA, and compelled an end to isolationism, President Roosevelt was able at last to use US power to come to the aid of those nations, such as Britain, at war with the totalitarian states such as Germany and Japan.

So for once, to say that December 7th was the day upon which the world changed forever, is not to exaggerate. We still live in the world that Pearl Harbor created.

We saw earlier that the Japanese had long debated whether to go north against Siberia or south-east into the Pacific, to create what they called a 'Co-Prosperity Sphere', or a Japanese overseas empire in all but name. Pearl Harbor was the result of the decision to take the fateful southern option. One of the key reasons for this is that Siberia was thought at the time to have no natural resources (even today its oil is difficult to extract) whereas areas such as Malaysia and Indonesia, then ruled by the British and Dutch respectively, had the vast amounts of natural resources that Japan so needed. Japan had to import nearly 100 per cent of its oil and rubber, for instance. These European colonies had abundant supplies of these commodities.

So while we remember Pearl Harbor, it was not just there that the Japanese were attacking. They had already seized Indochina (today's Vietnam, Laos and Cambodia) from the French Vichy regime, and now they launched a campaign of gigantic overseas conquest. But to achieve this it was vital to neutralise or eliminate the threat of the American fleet. This is what happened on December 7th, when waves of Japanese planes took off from their aircraft carriers in the Pacific. The actual raid itself lasted just an hour and a quarter, with very few losses to the attacking side.

The USA lost four battleships completely, four were damaged and eleven other ships sunk or hit badly. Many aircraft were also destroyed and some 2,403 died in the attack. Just under half the dead were from one battleship, the USS *Arizona*, which sank.

Thankfully, however, the Japanese were not able to destroy any of the key American aircraft carriers – since none of them were there! Because it was to be aircraft carriers rather than the behemoth-like new battleships that were to be the main weapons of war in the Pacific in the next four years, this was fortuitous. The USA had been damaged but was very much alive to fight another day.

There are endless conspiracy theories about Pearl Harbor, usually along the lines of Roosevelt and Churchill suppressing information about the impending attack and doing nothing about it in order to get the USA into the war. As with all such theories, they do not stand up to historical scrutiny. Japanese diplomatic codes had been broken by the USA but not so many naval codes were deciphered. And the USA were expecting Japanese aggression – but against the European colonies, as was indeed the case – not against their own territory. Incompetence is not glamorous as a reason for major events, but all the genuine enquiries into Pearl Harbor suggest that just such lack of co-ordination was far bigger a reason for the unexpected attack than any designs Roosevelt had to enter the war.

BLITZKRIEG IN THE PACIFIC

December 8th 1941–January 31st 1942

The Japanese *blitzkrieg* from December 8th 1941 until around March 1942 was their most successful moment of the war. It was their equivalent of the effortless German conquests of the Low Countries and France in 1940, and in many ways as misleading a guide as to what would happen as Hitler's triumphs had been.

Hong Kong was captured within ten days, by December 18th. Thailand was taken quickly and soon the Japanese were attacking the British possessions of Burma and Malaya (in those days separate from other parts of today's Malaysia). On December 15th oil-rich Borneo was taken, before the British and Dutch defenders were able to destroy the wells. The Japanese sank two key British battleships, the *Prince of Wales* and the cruiser *Repulse* on December 10th. Churchill was horrified and shocked by these rapid disasters – he had not realised that even modern battleships such as the *Prince of Wales* could be taken easily by aircraft attack from enemy ships.

Then came the attacks on the Philippines (which we will see separately) and on the Malay Peninsula.

Australians still feel bitter about this part of the war, as do British people in Cambridge, since the defenders of British imperial possessions were a mix of Australian, Indian and Cambridge Regiment forces. With just two divisions the Japanese should have been crushed by superior British and Empire forces. But using bicycles and by gaining superiority in air power (the RAF was mainly elsewhere), the Japanese were able to advance an astonishing 400 miles in fewer than two weeks. One writer has called this 'the greatest triumph of Japanese arms during the whole war'. But as another author, Correlli Barnett, reminds us, in terms of manpower Churchill's thoughts were very much still in North Africa and in the fight with Rommel, not to mention the need to defend Britain itself in case Hitler should ever change his mind and restart Sealion.

But we should not forget that while ten Japanese divisions were involved in the attack south (including the invasion of the Philippines), no fewer than twenty-five remained fighting in China. The Japanese would soon be fighting a war in three places – South East Asia, China (where they had been at war since 1937) and against the might of the USA in the Pacific. They might be winning for now but long term the dangers of overstretch would soon become apparent.

THE FALL OF SINGAPORE

February 8th–15th 1942

Churchill described the fall of the island city of Singapore in February 1942 in his war memoirs as one of the worst defeats of the whole conflict. This was certainly true from the British and Australian viewpoint, since no fewer than 130,000 troops from the United Kingdom, Australia and India were captured by the victorious Japanese: 80,000 of these were from Singapore itself; and 50,000 from the mainland defence of the island. British supremacy in Asia was never the same again, and the absurd notion of white superiority over 'Oriental' races, always mythical, was dealt a fatal blow.

Singapore was surely always indefensible from a major land-based attack, and as the Japanese had conquered vast swathes of South East Asia, including the Malay Peninsula, the likelihood that Singapore could survive a siege was thus slim. Nonetheless, as the premier British naval base in the Pacific, its prestige made it necessary to attempt to hold. Even within a few weeks of the collapse, the 18th Division, consisting mainly of troops from the eastern part of England, was sent to try to shore up the already shaky defences of the island.

Singapore was now an independent country in its own right. It was separate as a colony under the British from the rest of the Malay Peninsula and was mainly inhabited by people of Chinese ancestry. Its island status is theoretical, since only a very few miles separate Singapore over the Straits of Johor from the Malay mainland. But the British commander, Lieutenant General Sir Arthur Percival, had done little to make sure that the landward side of the island was properly fortified.

So when the Japanese invasion force attacked on February 8th, under General Tomoyuki Yamashita, the omens were not good. There was virtually no air force with which to combat the intruders, and so the Japanese forces were able to land without any difficulty. On February 15th General Percival was forced to surrender, with ignominy. One of the Australian commanders, General Gordon Bennett, disgraced himself by escaping on one of the last boats out, leaving his wretched troops behind to suffer four years of barbaric Japanese prison camp.

Almost as soon as the conquest took place, the Japanese launched a major massacre of tens of thousands of ethnic Chinese. Their sorrows were thus even greater than those of the large numbers of European civilians also captured by the victors. Yamashita would be hanged in 1945 for this atrocity. It shows that the idea some Asians possessed of their fellow Asiatic races combating a common European enemy was nonsense, since the Japanese treatment of Chinese people, especially in mainland China itself but also in all parts of the Chinese diaspora such as Singapore, was utterly cruel and inhumane. It is not surprising that, decades later, the Chinese people still regard Japan, and the Japanese effective refusal to deal with the past, with the gravest of suspicion.

THE BATTLE FOR THE PHILIPPINES AND THE BATAAN DEATH MARCH

December 8th 1941–May 6th 1942

The British humiliation in Singapore in February 1942 was matched by an equally great American loss in the struggle to save what was then the US colony of the Philippines from Japanese invasion.

The USA realised that to defend the entire Philippine archipelago against the Japanese would be all but impossible. In charge of American and Filipino forces was the retired Chief of Army Staff General Douglas MacArthur who withdrew effective forces to the island of Luzon. But even this was to prove a forlorn hope. The USA, expecting civilised behaviour from the Japanese, declared the capital city of Manila an 'open city' (i.e. one that should not be fought over). The Japanese ignored the request and bombed much of the US–Filipino defences into rubble.

The majority of the American-Filipino army, or what was left of it, now retreated to the Bataan Peninsula, and to the island fortress of Corregidor, both places not far from Manila. But the Americans could not be defended from vicious tropical diseases, and many succumbed to dysentery and malaria.

Roosevelt now decided to recall MacArthur to move to set up Allied resistance in Australia. This was not as safe a venue as might be thought – some Japanese submarines managed to reach as far as Darwin, in Australia's Northern Territories. MacArthur fled Corregidor on March 12th and arrived, with massive publicity, in Australia, where in 1945 he proclaimed his soon to be legendary words: 'I shall return.'

But meanwhile thousands of American and Filipino troops were still holed-up in Bataan and some 2,000 in particular in Corregidor. The situation proved hopeless, despite the bravery of the defenders. On May 6th the fortress at Corregidor was forced to surrender.

Japan did not recognise the concept of surrender, since in Japanese society and culture such an act was deemed too shameful even to contemplate. Consequently, as tens of thousands of British and American prisoners of war discovered, the Japanese did not treat those who surrendered to them according to the laws of war or the Geneva Conventions. (In fairness it should be said that the Germans treated only Western prisoners of war properly – captured Russians were dealt with perhaps even more barbarically than the Japanese behaved to Western captives.)

Consequently thousands of Filipinos were slaughtered then and there, stabbed to death with bayonets. The others, including the Americans, were taken on a sixty-five-mile walk that has become infamous as the 'Bataan Death March'. It is reckoned that perhaps as many as 5,000 Americans were killed on the route to prison camp, and hundreds more were to die in captivity.

Japan was on a victory roll, but soon the USA would have plans to turn the tide.

THE BATTLE OF THE CORAL SEA

May 7th–8th 1942

With the fall of so much of South East Asia to the Japanese in late 1941 and early 1942, it looked as if their strikes against Western possessions in the region would be unstoppable. The next main target was northern Australia, where some of their submarines had already penetrated, and the inexorable progression of Japanese forces looked like the fall of dominoes, so fast was it toppling.

But, as Paul Kennedy reminds us, the further they reached with their conquest the longer their supply lines had to become and the further away from home bases they stretched. As with the Germans in Russia in 1941, what seemed like inevitable victory would soon come to a nasty halt.

And because of their attack on Pearl Harbor on December 7th 1941 they were not just fighting against completely overstretched and under-resourced Europeans. Now they were waging war against the rising might and determination of the United States, a nation intent upon revenge for the Pearl Harbor attack.

In the wider world the best-known US commander in the Pacific is General Douglas MacArthur. But in fact Roosevelt cannily split the Pacific into two theatres of war, of which MacArthur commanded only one. The other was under the authority of Admiral Chester Nimitz, a man not as prone to self-promotion and ruthless use of publicity as MacArthur. Nonetheless he was someone who many now reckon to be one of the greatest of all the commanders in World War II.

On April 28th Nimitz ordered ships to intercept a Japanese naval group coming towards Port Moresby in Papua New Guinea, the capture of which was vital to the eventual planned conquest of northern Australia itself. US Naval intelligence had not been able to decipher every Japanese naval code but they had been successful enough to find out where the enemy was heading. So as the Japanese steamed towards the Coral Sea, an American/Australian force was ready for them.

On May 7th the US launched the attack, sinking the Japanese carrier the *Shoho*. Until now ships attacked one another with battleship guns. But on the May 8th there took place what has been described as the first aircraft-carrier-to-aircraft-carrier battle in history. Planes from one side took off from aircraft carriers to attack the planes and ships of the other side. The USA lost the USS *Lexington* and the Japanese carrier *Shōkaku* was badly damaged. Over two days of hard fighting the USA lost 81 aircraft and the Japanese 105.

It can be disputed as to who actually won the battle as neither side conclusively prevailed over the other. Some think of it as a Japanese tactical victory but an Allied strategic victory, which might sound contradictory but is probably the best way to look at what happened.

But the main thing is that the Japanese were no longer invincible. They had inflicted damage on the USA but had also suffered major losses themselves. Port Moresby in Papua New Guinea had not been captured and the Australians were safe. The Japanese victory roll was over.

THE BATTLE OF MIDWAY

June 4th–7th 1942

The late Sir John Keegan, the Royal Military Academy Sandhurst lecturer, has described the Battle of Midway as 'the most stunning and decisive blow in the history of naval warfare'. While this may be slightly exaggerated, there is no question but that Midway was one of those pivotal engagements that deserve their great status. In just three days the American Navy was able to turn the tide of the war in the Pacific and put the Japanese on the defensive for the first time. The great Japanese admiral, Yamamoto, thought that it would be an historic encounter, and he was proved correct – but not as he had planned. No fewer than five aircraft carriers, eleven battleships and 5,000 troops were ready for the decisive engagement, which therefore made the Japanese loss all the greater when it happened.

Midway is in the middle of the Pacific – hence its name. The Americans knew that they were outnumbered (by about five to three), but they had two more carriers than either Yamamoto or the First Air Fleet Commander, Admiral Nagumo, realised that they possessed.

Hostilities began on June 4th, once more along the same lines as in the Coral Sea, with ships not able to see each other but aircraft able to take off and attack one another's planes and ships. Initially the Japanese planes seemed to outclass those of the US Navy, so Nagumo was thus lured into a sense of fatal complacency. This meant that when the next wave of US planes came, the Japanese carrier fleet had no aircraft ready and airborne to intercept them.

US victory at Midway has been nicknamed a 'miracle' but this is perhaps unfair on the bravery of the American pilots who were able successfully to take advantage of the situation and bomb the key ships of the Japanese fleet into oblivion, which is what now proceeded to happen.

Within no more than five minutes the US pilots were able to destroy four Japanese carriers, almost 300 planes and some 3,500 crew, who would thus not live to fly again.

Unlike Coral Sea this was a clear American victory. While it may not have been a triumph along the lines of Nelson winning Trafalgar in 1805 – which it would have been if Keegan's description as the greatest naval victory in history is right – it was unquestionably a deserved US and therefore Allied laurel. Another historian, Ewan Mawdsley, has suggested that it probably shortened the war in the Pacific by at least a year, and that argument makes complete sense.

VJ-Day – Victory over Japan – was still more than three years in the future. But one could say that Midway turned the tide, as never again would the Japanese be on a winning streak. Now the momentum had shifted permanently in favour of the USA. That would remain the case in the Pacific War right down until the surrender of Japan in 1945. The US pilots in Midway can join the 'Few' in the Battle of Britain as aircrew who made a critical and all-important victory possible at a pivotal point in the war.

PART THREE: I

1941–1942

The Eastern Front

THE SECOND BATTLE OF KHARKOV

May 12th–18th 1942

Following the successful defence of Moscow in December 1941, Stalin felt that anything was now possible. The counter-offensives launched against the Germans from December 5th onwards certainly ensured that the Soviet capital would not be captured. But the Germans amazingly managed to hang on, without being pushed back hundreds of miles, which is what Stalin rather arrogantly thought that the Red Army would now be able to achieve.

So by February 1942 there was a kind of stalemate on several fronts. Stalin had hoped not only to push back the Wehrmacht from the gates of Moscow in the centre, but also to relieve pressure on the sieges of Leningrad and of Sevastopol, and also to prevent the Germans from continuing their invasion south towards the oil fields in the Caucasus.

Needless to say, to accomplish all this was a very tall order. Since any admission of defeat was impossible, Zhukov was able to describe the Red Army attempts as a 'Pyrrhic Victory', which might be an accurate summary. For this time the entrenched German forces were protected by the slush, the infamous *rasputitsa*, and proved impossible to dislodge.

Stalin nonetheless wanted continuous attacks and one of these was the decision to liberate the key Ukrainian city of Kharkov that had been captured by the Germans the previous year. In charge were Marshal Timoshenko, and the Political Commissar and future General Secretary of the Communist Party, Nikita Khrushchev.

Unfortunately for the Red Army, the Germans were also planning an offensive, to be called Operation Blue, at which we will look later. As a result the attack was a disaster, with well over 170,000 Red Army casualties and the loss of vast numbers of brand new tanks. Both Timoshenko and Khrushchev wondered if Stalin would have them shot. In the end Stalin emptied cigarette ash on Khrushchev's bald head, to much merriment, and spared his life, a humiliation that Khrushchev never forgot.

Some 1.4 million Red Army soldiers lost their lives in the period between the ending of the siege of Moscow and the failure to liberate Kharkov. Thankfully for the USSR, this gigantic loss would be replaced, but it represents a failure to make a decisive breakthrough against the Germans. Years later, in his recollections, Zhukov was to blame the impetuosity of Stalin, and while Zhukov himself must bear part of the responsibility, nonetheless that is quite possibly close to the mark.

OPERATION BLUE

June 24th–November 28th 1942

In June 1941 Hitler had launched Barbarossa with the intent of wiping out the Soviet Union. But by April 1942 even he was getting more realistic about how much he could achieve in the vast expanses of the USSR. So that month he issued a new directive, ordering that the aim now was 'definitively to destroy any military strength remaining to the Soviets and as far as possible to deprive them of the most important sources of strength of their war economy'.

And economics was primarily what it was now all about. The Donbas region of the USSR had something like sixty per cent of all Soviet coal. The Germans also wanted the oil fields of the Caucasus and the seemingly attainable goals of capturing two particular oil-producing towns, Maikop and Grozny. These considerable supplies of oil would both deprive the Soviets of that essential commodity and more importantly still, hand it over to the Germans.

So Operation Blue was not a war of ultimate conquest but one of achievable goals – at least that was the plan.

For that reason, while the final conquest of Leningrad by Army Group North was still a German war aim, the main thrust of the June 1942 offensive would be neither there, nor with Army Group Centre, the armies that had narrowly failed to capture Moscow in December 1941. Now all the concentration would be on Army Group South, and the capture of as many of the key economic assets of the USSR as possible.

However, the Soviets had a different view, one with the very human story of indescribable bravery in the ruins and streets of Stalingrad. For them the central area of the front was still of critical importance, especially since Moscow was now a mere 100 miles from the front line. Not only that, but as subsequent events would prove, it was this central part of the front that was to be the quickest route to Berlin and to the defeat of the Third Reich.

Therefore well over 500,000 troops remained ready to defend the capital from German attack, and some 300,000 Red Army soldiers kept open the route to Leningrad hundreds of miles away near the Finnish border. When in November 1942 the gigantic Soviet counter-offensive began in Stalingrad, there were some 1,100,000 Red Army troops in the south and around 2,530,000 soldiers in the centre. Not even the desperate struggle for Stalingrad itself would alter these ratios.

To begin with, the offensive began very well for the Germans. At the Battle of the Don Bend the Red Army lost 370,000 soldiers and 2,500 equally irreplaceable tanks. This time too the Germans were able to capture Rostov on July 23rd. This was one of the most important cities on the River Don, and incidentally one with a much larger population than that of Stalingrad.

Stalin grasped the importance of these major Soviet defeats. So on July 29th he issued his soon to be legendary no retreat decree:

> This means it is time to stop retreating. Not one step backwards! This must now be our main slogan. It is necessary steadfastly, to the last drop of blood, to defend each position, each metre of Soviet territory, to hold every patch of Soviet soil, and to hold it as long as possible.

In fact Hitler now, once more, came to the Soviet Union's aid. Instead of keeping all his southern armies together, on July 23rd he split them into two groups. Army Group A would continue on from Rostov down through to the Caucasus, while Army Group B would attack Stalingrad, the vital arms manufacturing city on the Volga River.

With Army Group A – the direct command of which Hitler took over himself in September 1942 – success came, but at a slow pace. This was not so much owing to Red Army resistance but to the sheer scale of the geography. German troops made it to Mount Elbrus, the highest peak in the Soviet Union, and even reached as far as Grozny, only to discover that the evacuating Red Army troops had spiked the wells, making them useless. But now German supply lines were drastically over-extended, and the truly great Caucasus oil prize, the city of Baku, was still 350 miles distant.

THE SIEGE OF SEVASTOPOL

October 31st 1941–July 4th 1942

In their great sweep of conquests in 1941, the Germans not only failed to capture Moscow but also the vital Crimean naval fortress of Sevastopol, a place familiar in history from the Crimean War in the 1850s.

Now the Germans were determined to make up for lost time. Operation Blue was the main offensive, but the attack on the Crimea was also vital. However, since Turkey had valiantly and prudently managed to stay neutral, the capture of the fortress still did not permit naval passage through the Mediterranean into the Black Sea, since the Turks maintained the rights to prevent navies going through neutral Turkish territorial waters in the Bosphorus and thence the Black Sea.

But the Red Air Force had been able to use Sevastopol as

a base from which to bomb the Romanian oil fields, a critical source of supply for Germany who relied very heavily on oil from that region. Hitler was hoping that his forces would get down to the Caucasus, to massive oil fields such as Baku, but for the time being Romania was all-important and the Soviet ability to hit the latter's oil wells was thus essential.

By May the Red Army ability to send ground reinforcements to defend Sevastopol had been cut off. On June 7th the land offensive began and within a month of close and often brutal fighting, the Germans finally prevailed. The Red Army had sustained not only heavy losses but also a major strategic blow.

And it is important to remember that not only German troops were involved but substantial numbers of Romanians as well – the Axis invasion of the Soviet Union was a fully international affair.

PART THREE: II

1941–1942
The War in North Africa

THE FALL OF TOBRUK

June 21st 1942

In 1941 the key Libyan port of Tobruk had survived a 240-day siege by Axis forces, with its intrepid British Empire defenders holding out against all the odds.

But in June 1942 Rommel and his *Afrika Korps* launched a massive counter-attack against British and Allied forces in North Africa. In a series of successful encounters, the beleaguered British-based Eighth Army was slung out of Libya and back onto Egyptian soil. All their extraordinary gains in 1941 were undone by Rommel's successes.

One of his victories was the final capture by German and Italian troops of the goal that had eluded them for so long, the port of Tobruk.

Not only was this a major achievement for Rommel, but a

devastating blow for the Allies. Some 30,000 and many more South African troops were captured by the Axis, following close on the much bigger disaster in Singapore earlier in the year. Worse still in some ways was the fact that when the news came through of Tobruk, Winston Churchill was in Washington DC with Roosevelt, involved in delicate negotiations about long-term Allied strategy. It was a humiliation to have to suffer news of this loss in front of the Americans.

But the cloud most assuredly had a silver lining. General George C. Marshall, the outstanding American Chief of Army Staff, immediately offered the British as many top quality tanks as they would need in North Africa with which to beat the Germans back. This generous offer came too late to save the careers of those British commanders whose lack of martial prowess enraged an embarrassed Churchill. But it meant that when General Sir Bernard Montgomery took control of the Eighth Army later that year, he had, from the USA, all the possible new equipment that he could possibly have wanted. Humiliation at Tobruk contributed directly to victory in the autumn of 1942 at Alamein.

THE FIRST BATTLE OF EL ALAMEIN

July 1st–27th 1942

Not many people today realise that there were *two* battles of El Alamein, and that 'Monty' (General Sir Bernard Montgomery, later Field Marshal Viscount Montgomery *of Alamein*) was commander in the second one but not in the first.

On May 28th Rommel's forces began a major offensive at the Gazala Line in Libya, and were soon vanquishing their enemies everywhere – including, as we saw, the iconic capture of Tobruk, for which Churchill himself was censured by many in the House of Commons for failing to get a grip on the war.

By July Rommel was feeling very confident that Cairo would soon be his, something that terrified the British inhabitants of the Egyptian capital. (The fear felt by many of them is portrayed vividly in the novels by Olivia Manning, televised as *Fortunes of*

War, with Emma Thompson and Kenneth Branagh.)

However, in order to get to Cairo by the most expeditious route, the Germans and Italians had to pass through a gap in which was situated a small place called El Alamein, not far from Alexandria. Andrew Roberts has nicely described it: 'set in hundreds of miles of absolutely nothing.'

By this time the British Commander-in-Chief Middle East, Sir Claude Auchinleck, had sacked the inefficient Eighth Army commander, General Ritchie, and had bravely taken direct control of that army himself. On July 1st, when the Axis forces reached El Alamein, the British and Empire forces were there and waiting.

As Roberts suggests, the attack by the *Afrika Korps* was pure hubris, since they were by now as exhausted as the British and Allies. Auchinleck was able to counter-attack, and an on-off battle raged until July 27th.

In terms of outcome, the consensus seems to be that the first battle at El Alamein was a draw – neither side won. But Rommel's seemingly invincible juggernaut had been stopped. Cairo had not been captured.

This was good news for the British. Earlier in the year, Churchill had been embarrassed to be in Washington DC when the news of the fall of Tobruk had come. So he did not see it that way. Auchinleck was sacked, just as Wavell had been. It would take two men to replace his two commands. The original idea was to put General Richard Gott, a young commander with desert war experience, in as the new commander of the Eighth Army. He, in turn, would be under the overall command of General Sir Harold Alexander, Churchill's favourite general who was now Commander-in-Chief Middle East. But Gott was killed in a plane crash on his way to Cairo. So instead a general from Britain, with no desert experience, was placed in charge of the Eighth Army, General Sir Bernard Montgomery. Monty was made of sterner stuff and was, as we saw, exceptionally lucky because, by the time that he took command, the vital American supplies were starting to arrive. The war in the desert would now start to change.

PART FOUR: I

1942–1943
Allies Begin to Turn the Tide: The Eastern Front

STALINGRAD

August 23rd 1942–February 2nd 1943

Although well over three-quarters of the German forces fought against the Soviets on the Eastern Front rather than against British and American forces in the West, we do not know as much about the titanic struggle between the Wehrmacht and the Red Army as we should.

However the great battle and siege of Stalingrad is as famous throughout the world as it should be. So pleased were the British even during the war itself that they presented Stalin with a special Sword of Stalingrad in commemoration of the famous Soviet victory. Books such as those by Antony Beevor, and films such as *Enemies at the Gate*, have also given Stalingrad its full due as an encounter worthy of the attention paid to it.

Originally though Stalingrad should not have been besieged

at all. Hitler's main obsessions were economic, the breadbasket of the Ukraine to feed his troops and the oil of the Caucasus to fill his tanks with petrol. Gaining Stalingrad was thus intended as a move to capture a key town that would protect the even more important thrust to the south after he divided his forces on July 23rd.

Writers such as Philip Bell have suggested that the Germans could easily have occupied a position on the Volga River that would have prevented all Soviet ships and transport from getting through to Stalingrad. But it seems that it was deemed better – including by Hitler himself – for the actual city to be taken. Here one has to suppose that its very name – before 1925 it was called Tsaritsyn and many years later Khrushchev changed its name, again, to Volgograd – had powerful symbolism, as much for Hitler as for Stalin.

During the Russian Civil War both Stalin and Voroshilov, another important Bolshevik leader, had been instrumental in the defence of Tsaritsyn against 'White Russian' anti-Communist forces, and had held the town against all the odds. During the conflict, 1942–1943, Hitler often referred to 'Stalingrad', sometimes falsely to pretend that it had fallen completely into German hands. At the same time ghostly appearances of Stalin gained popular currency, equally fantastical but also sincerely believed. This then was no ordinary battle but an iconic struggle between the two dictators, and one which hundreds of thousands of ordinary people, from German soldiers to Russian civilians, paid for with their lives.

(Even to this day it remains unclear exactly how many suffered and died in the five main months of the siege – Antony Beevor's

book *Stalingrad* has an appendix that tries to come to grips with
the likely actual numbers. Let us just say that a great number of
people died.)

The German commander, Friedrich von Paulus, was a brilliant
staff officer. But he had never commanded so much as a division,
let alone a vast army group. (As well as the German Sixth Army
there were many Romanian and other Axis forces under his
authority.) So important however did Stalin understand the
situation to be that he put Zhukov in charge, his best general.

The siege of Stalingrad can be broken up into three bits: (a)
before mid-November; (b) Operation Uranus, the Red Army
encirclement operation, which has its own entry; and (c) the
fighting with the Axis forces stuck inside the city from late
November to the German surrender on January 31st (the extra
few days being those of desperate stragglers fighting it out to the
end).

The fighting began on August 23rd, when elements of the
Sixth Army entered the city, after a long period of Luftwaffe
bombardment. Von Paulus had told Hitler that it would take
ten days actually to take the city, and then around a fortnight
to consolidate the German hold. However, given the ferocity of
Soviet resistance, this date soon became meaningless.

Historians writing about the siege after the cinema release of
the film *Enemies at the Gate* all point out that on the Soviet side,
not all the fighting was actually in the city itself. There were no
fewer than seven armies in and around the city, of which just
one, the 62nd Army (under the command of General Vasily
Chuikov), was actually involved in the street-by-street fighting
which has become so famous.

One could argue that by mid-November there was an effective stalemate: the Germans were inside the city and hard to dislodge, but the Soviets were fighting back and impossible to expel.

This is why Uranus made the difference – aid to the Sixth Army now became impossible. And as we saw, in any case Hitler did not want the German troops trapped inside the Stalingrad *kessel* to escape, as would have been the most prudent course. When he ordered Manstein to fly to the region to deal with the situation, in what became known as Operation Winter Storm (December 12th–23rd 1942), it was to break through into the city rather than to enable the Sixth Army and the various Romanian allies to break out.

Hitler also asked Goering to use the Luftwaffe to drop much needed supplies into the Sixth Army. Goering, rashly as usual, promised that his forces could deliver the necessary aid. However this was pure hubris, since the Luftwaffe not only had to fight the Red Air Force, but also the hideously adverse winter weather conditions. Not surprisingly, given these odds, the Luftwaffe lost some 500 transport planes to snow and gunfire, and the rescue attempt proved to be a costly fiasco.

Winter Storm was equally disastrous – not even a commander as adept as Manstein was able to break the Soviet stranglehold. Following this major loss the Soviets then launched their own offensive, Operation Ring, on January 10th, and this devastated the newly patched-together Army Group Don under Manstein's leadership. In addition the Hungarian and Italian forces on the outskirts of Stalingrad were swiftly crushed – most of the Italians cursed Mussolini, as they had never wanted to be there, so far from home, in the first place.

(It has also been pointed out that the Italian forces would have been far better off fighting in much better weather conditions under Rommel in North Africa. Mussolini's quixotic gesture in sending so many Italian troops to the Eastern Front was to cost him and eventually the Axis in general very dear.)

So by mid-January the beleaguered Sixth Army and its unhappy Romanian cohorts were now no less than 200 miles distant from the nearest major Axis armies.

Hitler refused all pleas for the entrapped Germans to break out. For him it was all a matter of iron will. But given the extreme cold conditions, the exhausted and seriously frostbitten Sixth Army were now utterly lacking in such determination.

Then on January 30th Hitler took the odd move of making von Paulus a full Field Marshal. The justification for this is that no Prussian or German Field Marshal had ever surrendered, so by this move, either von Paulus would win, or, more likely, kill himself rather than face the ignominy of defeat.

Von Paulus was not the stuff of which suicides are made, however. The very next day he surrendered to the Red Army, January 31st 1943. A few stragglers fought on until February 2nd but essentially on that day an enormous German army surrendered. It was a cataclysmic defeat for the Third Reich and personally humiliating for Hitler. It is significant that when the tenth anniversary of the Reich was celebrated, it was Goebbels who read out a speech by Hitler, rather than the Führer himself broadcasting to his own people.

The fate of the captured Germans was terrible. Many died in captivity and others suffered in Soviet prison camps, in dreadful conditions, well into the 1950s. Von Paulus himself lived on, in Soviet-controlled East Germany, the German Democratic Republic (the DDR), until his death in early 1957, just over fourteen years after his surrender in 1943.

Zhukov, by happy contrast, was made a Marshal of the Soviet Union, the very highest rank in the Red Army, for his glorious achievements. For him, albeit with a few small hiccups, it would be triumph all the way to Berlin in May 1945. The other main Soviet commander, General Alexander Vasilevsky, was also made a Marshal, and he too would have a successful war ahead of him. It would not be all plain sailing, but the Red Army was now on its own victory roll, from January 1943 to VE-Day just over two years later.

OPERATION URANUS

November 19th–23rd 1942

Operation Uranus, while unfamiliar to many of us in Britain or the USA, has also been described as *the* turning point battle in the Second World War. It enabled the Red Army completely to encircle the German Sixth Army holed-up in Stalingrad, along with the other Axis armies, and in effect prevent the other Wehrmacht forces from coming to the rescue of their surrounded colleagues.

So many battles have been nicknamed as pivotal or vital or game-changing that it is risky to take sides and choose a particular engagement as worthy of such status. But one can safely argue that Uranus was without question *one* of the most important of the war. The Germans suffered a cataclysmic defeat and there is a very real sense that afterwards they were never quite the same again. It would take over two-and-a-half further years for Berlin to fall and for the Third Reich to crumble, but one can say that the writing was now firmly on the wall.

Essentially Uranus was what the Germans called a *kessel* or cauldron-battle of envelopment, when one army surrounds another and makes it impossible to escape. This time however the encirclement was being done by Red Army troops to a German (and Romanian) force. There were two main Soviet army groups, one coming from the south, the other from the north, the two meeting up at the town of Kalach, a city on the River Don. Now the Sixth Army was seventy-five miles distant from the Wehrmacht forces under the control of Field Marshal Manstein, whom Hitler had dispatched urgently from the Leningrad siege to try to make the best of the situation for the Germans.

The rest of the story is best told in the account of Stalingrad. But it is interesting to reflect that now there were two armies forbidden by their political leaders – Hitler and Stalin respectively – to retreat from any positions that they held. Some have argued that von Paulus, the unfortunate Sixth Army commander, should have tried to evacuate as many of his forces as possible on or before November 19th. In normal strategic circumstances this would have been the most sensible thing to do. But normality did not apply either to German or Soviet armies, and even down to the very end of the war in 1945 German officers were obeying Hitler, however crazed the instructions might appear to be. Similarly the Red Army now had NKVD 'blocking divisions' that would arrest or shoot troops retreating or fleeing from the battle. This would be a very different kind of war from the one fought in the West.

OPERATION MARS:
RUSSIA CENTRAL FRONT

November 25th–December 20th 1942

The Soviet offensive named Operation Mars in late November 1942 has always been a controversial series of battles. Some historians, such as the US Army's main specialist in Soviet military history, David Glantz, claim that it was a full-blown attack in its own right. Others, however, feel that it was a very bloodthirsty diversion from Stalingrad, where the much more important Soviet counter-move Operation Uranus was launched effectively at the same time.

The official aim was to attack the German Ninth Army in the area of the Rzhev salient in the Wehrmacht's Army Group Central region. Some six Soviet armies were used in the assault, but it was a complete disaster. Red Army losses were about 70,374 dead and around 145,300 wounded, a defeat that Antony Beevor aptly describes as a 'massive sacrificial tragedy that was kept secret for nearly sixty years'.

David Glantz has described it as 'Zhukov's greatest defeat'. Today Zhukov is regarded as perhaps the best of all the Allied commanders in World War II (albeit one able to have victories regardless of the cost to the lives of his men). So it is understandable that people would not want him to have a major scale loss.

However, new research suggests, Antony Beevor tells us, that the whole thing was a fix, but one arranged by Stalin and by the NKVD (Soviet intelligence) at the very highest levels, so much so that not even Zhukov knew what was happening in secret behind the scenes. Through a very highly placed agent sent by the NKVD to the Germans under the pretence of being a defector, the Wehrmacht was given advance details of the Red Army plan, so that the six armies attacking German lines could be defeated. It is certainly true that the Soviet Armies in Operation Mars were given less artillery ammunition that those participating in the even more important Operation Uranus, to lift the siege of Stalingrad.

However, it should be said that not all specialists agree with such an interpretation. The original plan for the Mars offensive was October, and the delay in launch was because the Russians suffered as much from the vagaries of the *rasputitza* as the Germans. The delay enabled the latter to increase their numbers of Panzer tanks, for instance, and to add a month of preparation to counter any attack that came.

But either way, whether diversion or failure, it did make a significant difference to German fortunes further south, especially at Stalingrad. Aid to the beleaguered Sixth Army there became much more difficult. And the Ninth Army, it has been argued, was in no fit state come 1943 to take part in Hitler's last desperate throw of the dice, Operation Citadel, which we will see later.

So Mars was a tragedy, but possibly one that in the end had good results.

OPERATION CITADEL AND
THE BATTLE OF KURSK

July–August 1943

The German attack of July 1943, Operation Citadel, and the massive Soviet counter-attack, based in Kursk, are two intertwined military operations. So I am giving generic dates of simply July–August, since it was during those two critical months that the overall conflict was fought.

By now it was evident that the Germans could not beat the Soviet Union. However, if the new thesis that such an outcome was doomed from the start is true, then what the titanic events of 1943 do is to prove the full truth of that argument.

However, the Germans did not concede that they had lost the war. Even after Stalingrad they were still able to make gains and to hold on to gigantic swathes of territory. In February 1943, for example, they were able to retake the key city of Kharkov in what is now the Ukraine, wiping out some twenty Red Army divisions in the process.

As Mitchell Bard has written, 'The fact that Germany had recovered the initiative and appeared far from beaten alarmed Stalin, who now realised the war, and danger to his regime, was far from over.'

Stalin now decided to go for patriotism, and for *Russian* patriotism in particular. (Norman Davies and others remind us that much of the devastated area of the USSR was in fact ethnically Ukrainian and Belorussian.) The Russian Orthodox Patriarch, a symbol of the Tsarist past, was now reinstated in full glory in Moscow. Officers were also reinstated as a class in the Red Army having been abolished as old-fashioned after the Russian Revolution, and they could wear distinctive epaulettes, hitherto taboo.

More importantly he agreed with his main commander, Zhukov, that a war of attrition against the Germans was now the only possible way forward. As we saw, while millions of Soviet soldiers were dying, at least the USSR had the population to replace them – the Germans did not have such an option.

So two quite separate campaigns now evolved. One was the German attempt to kick-start their war, and wipe out as much of the Red Army, especially in the Kursk salient, as possible. For the Soviets, it was to wear down the Germans to unacceptable losses and then be ready to launch a massive counter-offensive that could take them all the way to Berlin.

This was one set of giants against another. By the time that battle commenced, on July 5th, both sides had been digging in and preparing for this existential encounter for months. Around

780,000 German forces faced a Soviet army of no less than 1,900,000 Red Army troops, with thousands of miles of trenches ready to receive the assault from fifteen German Panzer divisions with some 2,500 tanks. Some 300,000 civilian conscripts had been drafted by the Red Army to dig the defensive systems, and the longer that the Germans delayed, the stronger the Soviet defences were able to be.

(These figures are much larger than in some popular works. Exact numbers are notoriously difficult to find in parts of the Second World War, and I have taken the higher figures from books I have found to be reliable. Readers will find a wide variety of statistics when it comes to army numbers or casualties, especially in places such as the Eastern Front.)

To give some idea of the scale, there were some *six million* Red Army troops altogether by this time, over double the amount that had existed and been effectively wiped out back in 1941. The Nazis could produce nowhere near that number. They now had to recruit, especially for the *Waffen-SS* divisions, people from suitably Aryan-compatible races. But, by the end of the war, even French recruits or Bosnian Muslims were deemed suitable, people from very different racial profiles from that believed in so fervently by the Nazis.

At Kursk the *Waffen-SS* were impeccably Germanic, with divisions such as the *Liebstandarte Adolf Hitler* and *Das Reich*, both of which would become increasingly notorious as the war progressed.

Hitler had proclaimed, with characteristic hubris, that the inevitable German triumph at Kursk would 'shine like a beacon around the world'. By this time the Third Reich was having the danger of considerable overstretch, because simultaneous with Operation Citadel in central Russia was the now urgent need to send a German army to Italy to stop the Western Allies from conquering that country after the Allied landings in Sicily. Now the Reich really was having to fight a two-front war. Hitler's generals had wanted the battle in Russia to begin in March, which might have been logistically possible, and it was very much his decision to delay Citadel's launch.

Much of what follows is complex, as there were three operations taking place. Thankfully for those wanting more detail, Antony Beevor's chapter in his book on *The Second World War* is invaluable for sorting out who exactly was fighting whom, where and when, especially since the different fronts included quite an extensive area. Kursk was simply the town where the Red Army salient stuck out the most and the battles that now raged were over a much wider region of Central Russia.

As Beevor writes, the battle that began on July 5th with the German assault 'resembled a medieval clash of armoured knights. Neither artillery nor aircraft could help either side, so mixed up were the forces. Formation and control was lost on both sides, as tank fought tank at point-blank range'. The din was overwhelming and some of the casualties were soldiers going out of their minds because of the sheer noise and pandemonium that the clashes created.

The northern Soviet counter-offensive was Operation Kutuzov, named after the heroic Russian general of 1812, and it began on July 12th. In the south it was called Operation Polkovodets Rumyantsev and was launched on August 3rd. There were several Soviet Red Army groups, and as can be seen from their size –

nearly two million troops spread over the different Groups – the Soviets had overwhelmingly the superior numbers.

Kursk has been described as the biggest tank battle in history, and it is this medieval image, which Beevor so brilliantly conjures up for us, that gives us our main impression of the battle. There was a major aerial combat as well, with several Luftwaffe groups duelling in the skies with the Red Air Force. War aces on both sides scored major hits against each other's forces. Some 4,000 planes flew in all, and the Germans lost around 1,400 of them. In the varied engagements they also lost up to 3,000 tanks or more. Since German production capacity back in the Reich was increasingly limited, these were not machines that could be replaced. (Indeed some of the SS Divisions already had to use captured Soviet T-34s, as they had not enough of their own.)

Wikipedia gives Kursk as a decisive Soviet victory. In some ways this is fair, as they were unquestionably the overall winners, if all three different fronts are taken into account. Kharkov, for example, was taken for the fourth and final time, by the Red Army, and never again was the Wehrmacht able to launch a campaign of even remotely similar size against the Soviet Union. The author of the *Complete Idiot's Guide to World War II* writes: 'from that point on, the Russians seized the initiative, and did not let up until reaching Berlin.'

All this is true, but we should remember that the Soviet casualties in the three offensives were immeasurably higher than those of the Germans. Victory had come at a terrible cost.

In this piece the three battles – Citadel/Kursk, Kutuzov (against Orel) and Polkovodets Rumyantsev (known also by the Soviets as the Belgorod/Kharkov Operation) – should really be seen as one giant confrontation. It is possible to separate them, but that would be pedantic.

However, it is true to say that Citadel was a defensive operation for the Soviets, and the other two were offensives, and that it was the latter two which really allowed the Soviets to take the advantage. Although Red Army casualties were colossal – some estimate over 860,000 if such figures can ever be reliable – they really now were on a victory roll.

The Germans, by contrast, now had to retreat at least 150 miles, to what they now called the 'East Wall', a purely theoretical construct since no such fortifications actually existed. They were still on Soviet soil, but their days of advance were over. And by September 1943 they were back on the Dniepr River.

PART FOUR: II

1942–1943

The USA and United Kingdom: War Against Germany

THE SECOND BATTLE OF EL ALAMEIN

October 23rd–November 4th 1942

By August 1942, the new team, of General Sir Harold Alexander as Commander-in-Chief Middle East and General Sir Bernard Montgomery in charge of the Eighth Army, were now in place, following Churchill's reconstruction of the British and Empire armed forces in North Africa. New commanders also had new tanks, courtesy of the USA, as promised by General George C. Marshall in Washington DC. By now the Royal Air Force had critical air superiority in the region, thereby making Allied forces safe from German planes. Finally leaders like Montgomery knew how to use ULTRA properly, and so the British could plan their strategic moves in the full knowledge of where their enemy would be and when.

Rommel first tried his strength out against Montgomery at the

Battle of Alam Halfa, south of El Alamein, August 30th–September 5th. But his attack was unable to penetrate the now well-defended British lines and the Germans and Italians were repulsed.

Churchill had spent much of 1940–1942 incessantly badgering his commanders to get going, to invade or attack, and sometimes sent instructions down to as low as to battalion level. It was micromanagement, and while Churchill's overall grasp of grand strategy was impeccable, his ceaseless interference in operational issues regularly drove his commanders and military advisers to utter distraction.

Ironically therefore his new men in the field, especially Montgomery, refused to be railroaded by Churchill into making premature and probably rash decisions. Monty was by nature deeply cautious – a trait that would enrage his more gung-ho American allies later in the war. Like most of the commanders of his age and experience, he was deeply averse to casualties among his own men. Never again, a whole generation of generals felt, should there be the risk-taking carelessness with human life that had so marred the First World War, with the memory of the 57,000 casualties on July 1st 1916, the first day of the Battle of the Somme.

Monty is one of the most discussed and debated generals in British history. The Monty legend was created at El Alamein in October–November 1942, and so this is as good a place as any to look at one of Britain's most famous and also controversial military commanders. His views, methods and personality would all come into sharp focus from El Alamein right down to VE-Day in 1945. But without his decisive victory over the Germans in 1942, he would be as unknown as many of the other British and

Empire generals who lost their way in the desert in 1940–1942.

After 1945 Monty was the hero who could do no wrong but then, as always happens, revisionists entered the fray. In Britain but above all in the USA, with writers such as Carlo D'Este, Montgomery was savaged for being over-cautious, risk-averse, of somehow lacking grip. Monty was certainly not perfect, and it is perhaps true to say that other, sometimes lesser-known generals, such as Sir William Slim in Burma, were better.

As we shall see, Montgomery could be completely crass, was frequently insensitive to his more powerful American allies, and utterly self-promoting. But now books such as *Monty's Men* by John Buckley are rehabilitating, if not Montgomery himself, certainly the men who fought under his command, down to victory in 1945.

Much of the time he would use his natural predilection for showmanship – all planned down to the beret that did not belong to his regiment but which he wore anyway – to get the men on his side. Soldiers, everyone knew, would die. But Montgomery would take them into his confidence on what the battle would be about, and what their role in it would be. This, the average infantryman or tank trooper would feel, is a general who cares about us and wants as few of us to die as possible in order to achieve the goals that he has laid out. Monty, one could say, was a total egotist, but at least the men whom he commanded knew what they might die to accomplish.

Montgomery therefore stalled the politicians until he, as the commander of the Eighth Army, felt that he was ready. On October 23rd 1942 the Eighth Army guns blared out and one of the most famous battles in British history began.

The Desert Air Force had already been attacking German lines since October 19th, so that aerial as well as artillery bombardment were shaking up the enemy lines. This was a real difference from the Battle of the Somme.

Initially the attack went slowly. Rommel had been away in Rome when the actual engagement began, so he was obliged to fly back to the battlefield as fast as possible. Fortune was not with the Germans – one of their key commanders, Panzer General Gerhard Stumme, died of a heart attack. Then Hitler, whose micromanagement made Churchill's interference pale into insignificance, ordered Rommel to stand fast and not retreat.

By November 4th the British breakthrough had occurred. Many Italians surrendered, but controversially lots of Germans, Rommel included, escaped to fight another day. Montgomery has been blamed for this, and for not enveloping the Axis forces so as to make such an escape impossible. But as the war progressed, this is how the British increasingly fought the Germans – obtain the objective and then halt. On the one hand, this reduced casualties to one's own side (something that armchair generals fighting the battles decades later often overlook). On the other hand, critics are surely right to say that failure to take advantage of victory frequently leads to more casualties later on, as the enemy has not been vanquished utterly. Needless to say this debate has been going on for more than seventy years with no resolution in sight!

Antony Beevor, the former army officer turned historian, argues cogently that both the Desert Air Force and the Royal Navy played a major role in the El Alamein victory (which he dates as November 4th, excluding the follow-up fighting that lasted until November 11th). The Navy, aided by ULTRA, was able to sink key equipment deliveries planned for Rommel at a critical stage in the conflict, and air superiority proved a major asset to the forces on the ground.

Britain had won victories before November 1942. But these had always been countered by massive defeats, such as in Singapore or at Tobruk. In saying in his account of the Second World War that before Alamein the British never won a victory, Churchill is being unfair, but understandably so, since the losses considerably outweighed the successes. He is right to say though that after Alamein the British never really looked back. With the USA in the war they were on the winning side. Much of the victory was due to the superb American anti-tank weapons that British (and often Australian and New Zealand) troops were able to employ against German Panzers.

Compared to the kind of giant-scale epic battles being waged simultaneously on the Eastern Front, Alamein is a minnow compared to a whale. At El Alamein there were some 116,000 Axis forces, compared, for example, to over one million at Stalingrad (of which at least 400,000 were German). We are not really comparing like with like, something that it is easy for Western readers to forget.

But psychologically the British were surely right to celebrate the victory at Alamein with church bells. The major difference to winning the war would soon become apparent when a large America army landed in Oran, some distance up the North African coast. In time, especially a month or so *after* D-Day in 1944, there were to be substantially more US troops in Europe than those of Britain and the British Empire. However, Alamein made people in the United Kingdom *feel* different and considerably better. Victory in Europe would still be over two-and-a-half years in the future. But the endless cycle of defeats and strategic withdrawals was over. For the beleaguered British that was nothing but good news.

OPERATION TORCH

November 8th–16th 1942

One of the most remarkable things about the Second World War is how much the British and Americans agreed with each other. With the USSR, the USA and United Kingdom often had to walk on eggshells, since no one ever told Stalin what to do. As the war progressed Churchill found himself increasingly locked out of a closer relationship building up between the two major players, Roosevelt and Stalin, much to the British Prime Minister's sorrow. But well into 1943 the United Kingdom and its Empire were, to use an American phrase, 'big hitters' and Churchill's importance ranked accordingly.

One of the key decisions made by the USA even before Pearl Harbor was, as we saw, to put the defeat of Germany first, with priority over that of Japan. This was exceptionally good news for

Britain, whose very survival depended upon the crushing of the Third Reich. But it was an unpopular notion among many in the USA, who were both Japan-first supporters, and, in the case of several leading American navy and army personnel, strongly Anglophobic as well. The folk American memory of the British as the historic enemy from whom the USA gained its independence in 1776 had not gone completely away.

Roosevelt, being an astute politician, realised this. In early 1942 he had a dilemma. His key military adviser, General George C. Marshall, the Chief of Army Staff, and one of Marshall's brightest aides, Colonel Dwight Eisenhower, had formulated a plan. Their idea enabled the USA and United Kingdom to eliminate Germany first, through a large build-up of American forces in Britain (BOLERO) followed by an invasion of the European mainland close both to the British coast and to Germany, in northern France. This is what in fact happened when D-Day began in 1944, except that in 1942 the exact landing spot had not been finalised.

However such a build-up would take a considerably long time, if anything like the amount of American troops necessary to mount a successful invasion could be transported across the Atlantic. Here we need to remember that the Battle of the Atlantic against the U-boats had not been won and would not be until well into 1943. And the invasion itself was therefore not scheduled until April 1st 1943.

(Marshall also had a plan called Sledgehammer of short-term aid to the USSR in 1942, should the Soviet Union be in imminent danger of collapse. This plan was always only a contingency, but many historians have misinterpreted it as an American desire to have D-Day in 1942, which it was not. Thankfully the book by Andrew Roberts, *Masters and Commanders*, lays this error to rest by showing at length what was always obvious from the archives.)

The British historically believed in what is called the 'peripheral strategy', of attacking the enemy indirectly. This annoyed the Americans considerably, since to them to attack the main enemy *directly* – as happened in June 1944 in Normandy – always made much more sense.

However Roosevelt realised that if he was to keep to the 'Germany first' strategy, he had to have American troops fighting Germans as soon as possible. The only place available in 1942 to accomplish this was in North Africa, where British and Empire troops were already engaged in fighting Rommel. Churchill, with his belief in the peripheral approach, favoured the USA backing the Eighth Army straight away, in a plan code-named Gymnast. The British generals, with their memories of the horrors of the Somme and of the deaths on July 1st 1916, were all terrified that an Allied invasion of mainland Europe in 1942 would be a bloodbath. Since very few American soldiers had landed by this stage, most of the casualties, they reckoned, would be British and not from the USA.

Roosevelt was normally someone who trusted his senior generals and admirals to get on with the job – he never micromanaged in the way that Churchill was prone to do. But with Sledgehammer he saw a political opportunity to enable American soldiers to fight the Germans as soon as 1942.

So with the new name of Torch, the first Americans arrived in North Africa in November 1942, around the same time that the Germans were fighting the British at El Alamein. Since this is a book about battles and not politics, we can say in brief that these landings were not problem-free. US troops were landing in an area controlled by Vichy France, and not a few of the French officers and colonial officials were loyal to Vichy and not to the Allies. Nonetheless the Americans landed, and would soon face the Germans for the first time. It would prove to be a sharp learning curve.

WINNING THE BATTLE
OF THE ATLANTIC

March–May 1943

The Battle of the Atlantic, in one sense, lasted most of the war, since there was hardly a time when German U-boats did not want to stop vital supplies crossing the Atlantic to reach Britain. Under such schemes as Lend-Lease the USA was supplying the British long before Pearl Harbor in December 1941. After the USA's entry into the war, most troops crossed the Atlantic by boat so that by 1942 people as well as goods were among the most important cargoes making the crossing. Not only that, but the USA was equally supplying huge amounts of war material to the Soviet Union, in the Arctic convoys, with some taking the long and exceptionally hazardous journey from the US East Coast to the freezing Soviet port of Murmansk.

It was even before becoming Prime Minister that Winston

Churchill, in March 1941, coined the phrase 'the Battle of the Atlantic'. And as historian Philip Bell has commented, it was an unusual war. Many convoys made it safely without attack, or as the expression went, 'happy is the convoy that has no history'. But as we know, thousands of ships were sunk and lives lost, and for such people an icy and watery grave was a terrible way to go.

The Germans used more than just submarines. The Luftwaffe was able to sink as much as 580,000 tons of shipping in 1940 and more than a million tons in 1941. But having said that, the dreaded U-boat, under the command of Grand Admiral Karl Dönitz, was the Axis weapon that the Allies feared the most.

(It seems that the Japanese submarine fleet was considerably smaller than its German counterpart, although the Japanese Imperial Fleet was massively bigger than the German navy. So the effective submarines in the Pacific were those of the Allies. But intrepid U-boats did get to all sorts of places, to African waters, for instance, as well as the Atlantic.)

In 1943 Dönitz was put in charge of the entire German navy. This was to prove a bad move, as he was thus less close operationally to his U-boat crews, just at the turn of the tide in the Atlantic struggle.

As *Engineers for Victory* by Paul Kennedy shows, one of the Allies' greatest assets was technology. But here some of the most famous breakthroughs did not give the advantage that legend suggests. This is especially true of the code-breakers at Bletchley Park. In 1941 they could read U-boat signals traffic, so steered the Allied convoys (many of which were Royal Canadian Navy, as well as British) away from the danger zones. But in 1942, when the USA entered the conflict properly, German naval signals proved exceptionally hard to break, and the convoys making the Atlantic crossing were therefore obliged to do so blind. And for some of the war, it was the Germans breaking the Allied convoy codes, thus giving them a technological edge.

So throughout the Atlantic campaign, right down until 1945, the main Allied defence was the same as it had been in the previous war, the convoy. In charge of this was Admiral Sir Max Horton, one of the most important but sadly less well-known commanders of the war.

The German underwater equivalent was the 'wolf-pack', groups of U-boats hunting for Allied shipping in packs, which were better able to sink them once discovered. They had considerable success, and thankfully for the British, Dönitz was not able to get the numbers of U-Boats that he wanted, not in fact until January 1943. By this time the number of Allied escort vessels had increased considerably, including four light aircraft carriers in late 1942.

Many writers have pointed out that logistics played an enormous role in Allied success – Richard Overy's classic book *Why the Allies Won* shows this very clearly. By 1942 the key development was the Liberty Ship, a simple craft originally based upon a British design, but, thanks to American money and ingenuity, produced on an epic scale by US shipyards: thirty-five vessels had been completed by the end of 1941 and by 1942 they were being churned out at the astonishing rate of no fewer than sixty a month (and perhaps more than even that as the war progressed). By 1943 American shipping production had reached an enormous six million tons for that year alone.

There was no way even remotely that the Germans could

match this. US factories were also thousands of miles away from Axis bombers, whereas their equivalents in the Third Reich were under threat of bombardment by Allied planes all the time. The sheer scale of US production capacity – hence Churchill's famous aphorism of the 'arsenal of democracy' – shows how simple building technology of the kind that could roll off Liberty Ships with ease made a crucial difference to the outcome of the war.

And with the Allied invention of the High-Frequency Direction Finders (nicknamed Huff-Duff from the initials HFDF) the technological breakthrough necessary to locate U-boats made a transforming difference. Huff Duff could pick up U-boat radio transmissions, and another invention, centimetric radar, could even find U-boats at night.

All this was coming at exactly the right time, since the Allied losses to German U-boats in 1942 had been catastrophic. Without the ability to destroy U-boats, as well as to find and avoid them, it would have been very hard to bring over the gigantic number of American troops and tanks necessary for the USA to play its full part in the war in Europe. In the spring of 1943 the situation for the Allies was looking dire.

So in May 1943 the Allies made the critical decision to take on the U-boats directly. In one famous convoy, ONS-5, around May 4th–6th, the Germans were able to sink twelve merchant ships. But they lost nine U-boats and a further five were badly damaged. The Germans called this 'Black May'. As Philip Bell comments, quoting another historian: '[in] one action the mystique of the Wolf Pack had been broken.' In a single fortnight (May 10th–24th) no fewer than thirteen U-boats were sunk, and seven more destroyed by Allied airplanes.

On May 24th Grand Admiral Dönitz was forced to order his U-boats to restrict their actions and geographical range. A delighted Admiral Horton told his Coastal Command forces on June 1st that the 'climax of the battle has been surmounted'.

The Battle of the Atlantic would not end until May 1945. But as Horton had realised, the balance of the conflict was now firmly in favour of the Allies. All that vital war material, and hundreds of thousands of US military personnel, were now able to cross the Atlantic. The U-boats would still have occasional successes, but nothing like as much as before. The bravery of the Allied crews, facing all the Arctic cold, and technology had combined to win.

THE DAMBUSTERS

May 16th–17th 1943

Winston Churchill was famous for his support of 'boffins', men who were often eccentric scientists who would come up with all sorts of strange ideas, many of which were actually workable and some of which might even have helped to shorten the war.

One such inventor was Barnes Wallis. The story of how he was able to develop 'bouncing bombs' that bounced on the water before bouncing up to hit and destroy their target is an iconic one for British people. Wallis was the archetypal lone genius battling against the Establishment to come up with a magnificent invention that does what conventional means can never achieve. (Proof of this is surely in the fact that although the commander of the raid Wallis made possible was given the Victoria Cross in 1943, it was not until 1968, a quarter of a century later, that Wallis was finally knighted.)

The British were very worried about the production capacity of the Third Reich factories in the Ruhr, the heartland then as now of German industry. As we have seen elsewhere, precision bombing was not exactly the strength of the Royal Air Force, and the more targeted bombing of the US Army Air Force, was riskier as they carried out their raids in daytime.

However, above many of the towns and factories in the Ruhr were three large dams – the Eder, the Möhne and the Sorbe. If they were broken, they would flood the entire area below.

Technology at the time did not enable Bomber Command to breech dams in the way necessary to empty and to destroy them. However Wallis came up with an idea, which he had tested on English lakes that caused the bomb (strictly speaking a depth charge) to bounce first on the water and then up inside part of the dam wall. This breeched the wall in a way that caused a detonation that destroyed the dam itself.

Needless to say, eccentric inventors were not the kind of person with whom Air Chief Marshal 'Bomber' Harris found much sympathy. However Wallis was able to go higher up and gained the support of Air Chief Marshal Sir Charles Portal, the Chief of the Air Staff. This enabled proper trials to go ahead, and a special air squadron, 617 of Bomber Command, to carry out the raid. In charge was the already famous Group Captain Guy Gibson, an ace with many decorations for bravery already to his name.

On May 16th–17th 1943 the raids finally took place at night. The first two dams, the Eder and the Möhne were completely destroyed, unleashing torrents of water down to wipe out the factories below. The Sorbe, however, was only lightly damaged.

The morale boost to Britain of this very daring raid was very considerable. The devastation caused had been immense. Gibson was awarded the VC and the 617 Squadron were nicknamed 'the dambusters'. Gibson's own book *Enemy Coast Ahead* created even more of a legend, although he himself was tragically to die young in a raid the following year. A bestselling book *The Dambusters* ensued, along with a very famous film in the 1950s, whose popular music added to the aura of the raid.

Not mentioned at the time, however, was the fact that 1,600 civilians lost their lives in the destruction of the factories. Worse still was that 1,000 of them were Soviet forced labourers, allies of the British held by the Third Reich in terrible conditions. Today raids that cause widespread civilian deaths as an inevitable part of the action are no longer permitted under the rules of war. Furthermore, the Germans raced all out to repair the damage and it was fixed by the end of the year.

The bravery of the raid, and the sheer genius behind the conception, however, live happily on in British folklore of the war, an iconic moment of the long six years of struggle.

OPERATION HUSKY

July 9th–August 17th 1943

The invasion of Sicily was the first time that Allied troops had fought the Germans on European soil since the USA entered the war. The codename was Operation Husky. The decision to do so was a victory for Churchill and the British doctrine of the peripheral approach. Many Americans would have preferred to be fighting the Germans in north-west Europe, but Roosevelt was able to assure his leading generals that he would no longer allow their British allies to postpone D-Day indefinitely: it would now be 1944 whether Churchill liked it or not.

On May 9th the Axis forces in North Africa were finally vanquished following the capture of Tunis on the 7th.

The agreement to go for Sicily had been made back at the

meeting, which Churchill and Roosevelt had in Casablanca in January that year. Roosevelt had there enunciated the doctrine of 'unconditional surrender'. This was controversial to some, since they argued – as others do today – that demanding surrender without preconditions would make the Germans fight all the harder. But Roosevelt had history on his side. The thoroughly conditional nature of the German surrender in 1918 meant that the German Empire had been conquered without having been invaded and crushed into submission.

Hitler would use this as the basis for his 'stab in the back' theory, that *true* Germany had been betrayed by worthless politicians and Jews. This of course was completely untrue, but very persuasive to millions of Germans who had been defeated but wanted a scapegoat. This time around Germany would be totally wiped out and had to be visibly crushed with none of the ambiguity of 1918. As it turned out, that was indeed the case in May 1945, and Roosevelt would be proved right.

The invasion of Sicily is now famous because of the amazing deception operation that the Allies mounted successfully to deceive the Germans into thinking that the invasion would take place somewhere else. A dead body – in fact that of a poor Welshman who had died – was placed by submarine on a beach on the Spanish coast. This body had false plans planted on it that led the Germans to believe that the real invasion would be hundreds of miles away in Greece.

The ingenuity of the British deception plan has become legendary. A film was made about it called *The Man Who Never Was* and recently there have been both a television documentary and book by Ben Macintyre entitled *Operation Mincemeat*. This operation was to deceive the Germans into thinking that the next Allied move, Husky, would take place not in Sicily but elsewhere. The peak of British deception operations was to come with D-Day, with the Germans absolutely convinced that the *real* cross-Channel invasion would come at Calais, not Normandy. From the Trojan Horse onwards, deceiving the enemy has often become an integral part of warfare, and Mincemeat was a classic example.

The invasion of Sicily itself began on July 10th, the small island of Pantelleria having already surrendered. The command structure would give rise to conflict. In overall charge was General Dwight Eisenhower, and under him, in command of the ground forces, was General Sir Harold Alexander, 'Alex', Churchill's favourite general, and someone who got on well with Americans. But the two army commanders, the British Eighth Army under General Sir Bernard Montgomery ('Monty') and the US Seventh Army under General George Patton, were not friends. Both Patton and Monty were natural showmen, each with extreme braggadocio, and highly competitive with one another. This rivalry would last until Patton's death very shortly after D-Day in 1945.

By this time German confidence in the ability of their Italian allies to fight Western forces was not high. So when 140,000 Allied soldiers landed on Sicily, there were substantial numbers of German soldiers there as well as Italian.

History is written by the victors, but in the case of battles in World War II different victors often have diverging accounts of what happened and why. British writers have tended to say that Monty had the hard terrain in Sicily, so naturally took longer to reach his objectives. American writers point out that a commander as naturally bold and self-confident as Patton was able to scythe through Axis forces and reach his destination in record time.

Either way, tens of thousands of Axis troops were captured – but over 100,000 were able to escape over the Straits of Messina to the Italian mainland, to fight another day. Some 20,000 Allied forces died in Sicily, a large number, though in comparison with the titanic battles in Russia being fought at the same time. The conquest of Sicily cost far fewer lives than the 800,000 Soviet deaths at Kursk.

There is, however, another way of looking at Sicily, and in a far more positive light. As one writer, Evan Mawdsley, points out, 'Allied amphibious warfare in Europe came of age'. All the techniques that were to be so successful in D-Day in June 1944 were in operation in Husky. The three services – army, navy and air force – all collaborated properly. Furthermore, each of the wonderful new types of landing vehicles proved that they worked in practice under enemy fire as well. One can say that landing in Sicily was an excellent dress rehearsal for the considerably bigger Normandy landings a year hence.

The other achievement was the overthrow of the Italian dictator Mussolini on July 25th. Frantic negotiations now began on a successor regime, one that would, it was hoped, join the Allies. But things were not to be that simple . . .

OPERATIONS AXIS AND AVALANCHE

September 3rd–16th 1943

On July 25th 1943 Mussolini, the Italian dictator had been deposed – even his son-in-law Count Ciano was against him. So too was Marshal Badoglio, the commander of the Italian forces, and King Victor Emmanuel himself, the head of state whose negligence of his duties to democracy in the 1920s had allowed Mussolini to become ruler in the first place.

There then followed what the Italians have called the 'forty-five days', or what one could with some justice name the most wasted days of the war. In essence the new Italian regime, realising the way that the wind was blowing, knew that the Allies were now certain to win. Badaglio and the others thus wanted to change sides. But they were also, and with good cause, scared witless of what the Germans would do. So they spent forty-five days dithering as to what to do next.

The Allies were naturally keen to enlist Italy on their side, as to have them as a friendly nation would have made the invasion of the Third Reich infinitely easier. The leading statesmen, meeting in Quebec for the QUADRANT conference, also felt that it was unlikely that the Germans would send troops further south than the area roughly forming a line going west to east from Pisa to Rimini. This would leave most of central and southern Italy in Allied hands.

However, Hitler had just lost the Battle of Kursk. He was enraged to think that he could be betrayed by the Italians, and naturally therefore feared that Hungary and Romania, both key allies of the Reich in the war in the USSR, might do the same.

So while Badoglio dithered, Hitler started to make active plans to make as much of Italy as possible a clean slate (*tabula rasa*). One of his best commanders, Field Marshal Albert Kesselring, was dispatched to the country to prepare the seizure of the Italian army, of the capital Rome and all else he could manage.

The Allies had not wanted to give Badoglio their secrets. So they themselves were somewhat dilatory and a vital opportunity was thus lost to capture the Italian Peninsula for the Allied cause. In addition, the Americans suspected, with good cause, that Churchill wanted to use the planned Allied invasion of Italy as a diversion from the D-Day landings he had promised for 1944 in France. They therefore insisted that he agree to a fixed date for north-west Europe in 1944 (originally for May, as we now know for June 6th). They would brook no more delays on what they felt would be the major operation of the war, the direct defeat of Germany itself.

With the Italians dithering and the Allies not wholly united, the Germans were able to take full advantage. The original plan for the Allies had been to drop the 82nd US Airborne Division in Rome, but there was concern that such an action would not have sufficient air cover from Sicily. This proved just as well, since on September 8th 1943 a German force captured the city, and much of southern Italy as well. Instead the 82nd Airborne were to be of better use in Salerno, as we shall see below.

The Nazi Operation Axis was for them a huge success, with treble the number of German troops now in Italy than before the Italian defection. Both Badoglio and the King were able to escape Rome only by a hairsbreadth.

So for the Allies now landing, they were to be against a major *German* operation, under Kesselring, one of the most popular commanders on that side. He had around 400,000 troops and some key SS units were transferred from the Eastern Front to Italy, to lend him a hand. His forces captured some 650,000 Italian soldiers, who now became German prisoners-of-war. None of these unfortunate individuals were treated well, and at least 50,000 or more of them died as slave labourers in the Third Reich. The novel *Captain Corelli's Mandolin* tells the tragic story of how no fewer than 4,800 Italian soldiers were massacred on the Ionian Island of Cephalonia by angry Germans in search of revenge against men they regarded as turncoats. The one piece of good news for the Allies is that much of the Italian navy was able to escape.

The British and Canadian forces landed on September 3rd, in Reggio di Calabria and in Taranto. Thankfully for them, they were able to do so without too much difficulty, as Operation Axis had not yet got fully underway.

The Americans and the other British forces had landed in Salerno, not far to the south of Naples, on September 9th, in Operation Avalanche. Commanded by General Mark Clark, they had landed after the Italian armistice on September 8th. (Italy formally became an Allied nation on October 13th, but at that time most of the Italian Peninsula was still in German hands.)

So for Clark's divisions, instead of grateful Italians they now faced heavily armed German forces. His forces were very nearly expelled from the beaches, so chaotic did the landing prove. Thankfully the Allied navies were able to come to the rescue, as did the 82nd Airborne, and a disaster was thus narrowly averted.

The Allies now had a toehold in Italy. But it would prove a very long slog to victory, and only at the end of the war itself, in a most controversial deal with the Germans, did the end come. But meanwhile the slow progress up the Italian Peninsula began.

PART FOUR: III

1942–1943
The War Against Japan

BATTLE OF GUADALCANAL

August 7th 1942–February 9th 1943

The struggle for the key for the strategic Pacific island of Guadalcanal, in the region of the Solomon Islands, took place over several months during 1942–1943. The main battles took place in November 1942, overlapping therefore with the titanic struggle on the Eastern Front in Stalingrad and with the British battle at El Alamein. The geographic distances between all these places show that the war was now truly global in scope, fully justifying the title of *World* War.

Many of these small islands (Guadalcanal, for instance are twenty-five miles wide and ninety miles long) were not so much important in themselves as in providing critically needed air/land/harbour bases for major operations elsewhere. In July 1942 the Japanese had intended to use Guadalcanal as such a base, so on August 7th the Americans attacked, using planes from three carriers and the US Marine 1st Division. Some of the smaller islands were easily taken, but the 16,000 US Marines who landed at Guadalcanal had a major assault on their hands.

Several naval battles now ensued as the Japanese tried to help and increase their forces on the island, with the Americans trying to prevent them. The Japanese supply ships were soon nicknamed the 'Tokyo Express' by the American forces. It took some time for the USA to gain superiority at sea, with the Battle of the Eastern Solomon Islands on August 24th enabling the Americans to sink some Japanese ships, and at the cost of twenty planes in comparison with the Japanese loss of three times as many.

However, and very importantly, the US forces were able to capture the airfield on Guadalcanal. (This was named Henderson Field for a US Marine Corps pilot killed at Midway.) So while the Japanese were able to get several thousand reinforcements onto the island, the Americans now controlled the air. Attempts by the Japanese in August–October to capture the airfield all failed.

However, a naval war of attrition now took place, not dissimilar to the war of attrition in the trenches in Flanders in World War I but thankfully with fewer casualties. On October 26th a vast Japanese naval task force of four carriers, nine cruisers and twenty-eight destroyers attacked the Americans, whose force had only half the number of carriers and destroyers. The US carrier *Hornet* was sunk and the carrier *Enterprise* seriously damaged.

However, it is significant that the Japanese were acting some 550 miles away from their main naval base in Rabaul. They were now in real danger of being overextended. Not only that, but

US Naval Intelligence had spotted a new and powerful Japanese force aiming for Guadalcanal. Although the naval Battle of Guadalcanal, November 12th–15th, resulted in the US suffering major casualties, with the loss of 400 sailors, the Japanese were obliged to withdraw, without having been able to get close to recapturing the island.

Effective fighting was over by December, though the formal Japanese surrender did not occur until February. For 1,600 or so US dead (mainly US Marines), the Japanese had lost 15,000 killed, 9,000 wiped out by disease and with 1,000 surrendering to the Americans. Some 13,000 Japanese managed to escape.

The Americans had won, and the Japanese had been forced to withdraw for the first time in the war. But the USA was beginning to find out the sheer cost of attacking islands, from the tiniest to the largest. The Japanese would not surrender and would fight to the bitter end. This was not how war was supposed to be. Michael Burleigh has made an excellent study of this in his book *Moral Combat*. Compared to the Axis, the number of atrocities committed by the Allies was minuscule. But the war in the Pacific dragged on. This led to ever increasing casualties among the US Marines. They noticed that the cause was the fanatical resistance of the Japanese defenders, who fought ferociously to the last man. This made the Marines feel that the Japanese were somehow less than human, and to an unspoken decision to kill the enemy rather than allow them to surrender. The final two-and-a-half years of the Pacific struggle would not be pretty.

THE BATTLE OF ATTU

May 11th–30th 1943

The Americans were deeply blessed that continental USA was not attacked during World War II. Pearl Harbor was of course in Hawaii, and several of the islands in the Pacific over which so much blood was spilt were US possessions. But because the mainland itself was unhurt – the Germans never quite perfected intercontinental range missiles, although it was not for lack of trying – the Americans were able to be, as Churchill described them, the 'arsenal of democracy'. British factories were flattened, the Soviets had to rebuild theirs beyond the range of German bombers, and production in Axis countries was subject to regular Allied bombardment.

However there is one small part of the main USA that *was* occupied by the Japan – some of the Aleutian Islands off Alaska.

Thankfully this did not last for long. In May 1943 an American invasion force occupied the Aleutian Island of Attu, expelling the Japanese. This was done at comparatively low cost to the liberators but at much higher cost to the occupiers, with nearly 3,000 Japanese deaths.

It seems strange that Japan never tried to invade the western parts of the USA or Canada via the Aleutian Islands, all the more so as that route was the main supply chain from the USA to the USSR via Siberia. But that could have been part of the issue, since the Japanese had signed a non-aggression treaty with the Soviets in April 1941, and the Aleutians were very close to Russian soil. In addition the weather in that region was totally unpredictable, so a seaborne invasion would have held potential perils for anyone aiming to use it.

In August 1943 the Aleutian Island of Kiska was simply abandoned by the Japanese, and so American soil was now safe against Axis invaders. Apart from a few intrepid German submarines off the East Coast in the Atlantic, the USA was safe from danger.

PART FIVE: I

1944–1945

The Western Allies in Europe

THE ANZIO LANDINGS AND MONTE CASSINO

January 22nd–June 5th 1944

The landings at the beach at Anzio, just south of Rome, on January 22nd 1944, should have led to a swift capture of Rome nearby. The Allies were able to achieve total surprise, with 36,000 of their troops landed very quickly. The aim was to outflank the German defensive Gustav Line and be able to attack them from both sides. This was the plan for Operation Shingle and it should have been an easy success.

But unfortunately the American commander in charge of the actual landings themselves, General John Lucas, proved rather cautious, and the breakout that had been planned was not achieved. Field Marshal Kesselring, one of the ablest German officers, was ordered by Hitler to hold his line at all cost.

Consequently the Allies were essentially stuck where they

were for the next several months. Rescue was difficult because the rest of the Allied armies in Italy were stuck on the wrong side of the Gustav Line.

In order to blast through the German defences from the Allied foothold in Naples, it was necessary to pass through a small town just north of Naples, on the route to Rome. This was Cassino, whose Benedictine Monastery was one of the glories of Catholic architecture, on top of the mountain – Monte Cassino.

This epic struggle, to capture the mountaintop, was to last for months, January 17th–May 4th. Many have commented that the Italian terrain was utterly inhospitable to invasion, and that the Italian campaign of 1943–1945 was the only place where the Allies found themselves fighting in conditions similar to those in France in the First World War. The defenders had strong natural advantages, and the Germans made full use of the opportunities that the countryside gave them.

It was one of the most international groups of Allied forces that took part. There were British, Americans, Free French, Poles, New Zealanders, Indians (from the British Raj) and Italian Royalist soldiers as well. The Germans had taken control of the monastery, and this was aggressively carpet-bombed by the Allies, destroying not only German emplacements but also centuries of history.

D-DAY

June 6th 1944

'We won the war in 1944 . . .'

This ditty from the 1950s encapsulates the view of many in Britain and the USA and other parts of the West that D-Day, the Allied invasion of the Normandy beaches in June 1944, was *the* event that changed the course of the entire Second World War. How often did one hear talks saying something along the lines of 'We did not win the war itself until May 1945, but the outcome of the war was guaranteed after D-Day'?

There can be not the remotest question but that D-Day was *one* of the most critical days in the entire war. PMH Bell, in his *Twelve Turning Points of the Second World War*, one of the key texts for this and many other works on the conflict, is surely right to include it in his list of twelve.

But note what he says when he quotes an un-named fellow historian as being right to claim: 'The struggle for Normandy was the decisive western battle of the Second World War, the last moment at which the German army might conceivably have saved Hitler from catastrophe.'

Although Bell does not say so in his own book, one can argue that the vital word in that sentence is *western*. We have seen titanic battles such as Kursk, where nearly a million Germans fought against nearly two million Red Army soldiers. D-Day was gigantic, the biggest ever amphibious landing in history, but *as a battle* it was on a smaller scale than many of the enormous encounters on the Eastern Front, some of which, like Bagration we shall look at elsewhere.

It is possible to look at D-Day or Overlord to use its actual correct codename, in another way.

Overlord and the successful invasion of Normandy was the day upon which democracy in the West was saved. Until June 6th 1944 Stalin had been arguing for a Second Front, to take pressure off the bloodbath in his own country. There had been continuous action here since the German invasion in June 1941. Now after D-Day the Nazis were obliged to face a genuine two-front war, in Central Europe against the Soviets and in north-west Europe against the British, Canadians and Americans.

But as many have pointed out Stalin could well have continued even without D-Day. He had received enormous Lend-Lease aid from the USA, and aid of a more limited kind from Britain itself. All those transatlantic convoys from the American East Coast to the Soviet Arctic were bringing the urgently needed supplies that the Red Army required to keep the fighting going, to have that critical logistical edge over the Germans. If he had needed to, Stalin could simply have kept going not until Berlin but until the Red Army reached Calais, and conquered the whole of Western Europe as well.

As Philip Bell concludes, such a nightmare does not bear thinking about. But it is the alternative, if by horrible chance, the Allies had either not launched D-Day or, as in Eisenhower's worst scenario, been blown apart on the beaches and failed.

We know in hindsight of course that D-Day was a success. Precisely because of the triumph of Overlord, the Germans were defeated within eleven months of the landings in Normandy.

(Those historians who so criticise the supposed slowness of the Western Allies in the downfall of Germany forget this. Victory by Christmas 1944 might have been a wonderful aspiration and a goal worthy of pursuit, but it was simply unrealistic. We should surely, as writers like John Buckley, in his groundbreaking study *Monty's Men*, be thankful that it took as little time as it did, rather than moan that eleven months was a long time.)

Therefore, Western Europe was safe for democracy. France, the three Benelux countries, the whole of Western Germany, and, thanks to Montgomery's speed of action in 1945, Scandinavia itself, all were liberated by the armies of countries that were indisputably and proudly liberal democracies. Stalin may have got his forces first to Berlin but Western Europe, the core of the future NATO and European Union in the 1950s, was freed by American, Canadian, Free French and British forces under Eisenhower.

This book has argued that in effect, in invading the Soviet Union in June 1941 and in declaring war on the USA in December

1941 that Hitler, by those two actions, lost the war. After those two decisions, victory for the Third Reich was impossible, and its defeat was eventually inevitable.

But D-Day was still vital. It not only gave the democratic West a crucial say in the peace that followed VE-Day, but also, by splitting the forces of Nazi Germany, enormously helped the existential and wholly brutal struggle between the two totalitarian states in the East, between the Third Reich and the USSR. It is certainly the case that eight-five per cent of Wehrmacht soldiers fought on the Eastern Front, rather than against the democracies in the West. But Germany, with its diminishing resources, was utterly ill-equipped to fight the two-front war that started on D-Day.

What is also interesting about D-Day, something that Churchill understandably played down in his memoirs, was that it happened at all. (David Reynolds, in his *In Command of History*, shows us how what Churchill wrote at the time in official documents, and what he chose to record in his subsequent *History of the Second World War* could, at times, be quite different.) Churchill's top scientist Frederick Lindemann (1st Vicount Cherwell) once let slip to General George C. Marshall, the US Army Chief, that he 'must remember you are fighting our losses on the Somme . . .' When the US Secretary for War, Henry Stimpson, was on a visit to the United Kingdom not long before D-Day, General 'Pug' Ismay, Churchill's personal Chief of Staff, told his distinguished American visitor the same thing – the 57,000 dead on July 1st 1916 at the Somme were singed into the consciousness of every British leader, civilian, one could argue, as well as military.

Churchill did, to be fair to him, confess in his history of the war that the night before D-Day he envisaged thousands of young Allied soldiers being slaughtered on the beaches of Normandy. While Churchill's own section of the Western Front had been comparatively quiet, he was more than aware of the carnage only a few miles from the trenches in which he had briefly served.

All the top British soldiers had similar memories. Field Marshal Sir Alan Brooke, the Chief of the Imperial General Staff, confided in his diary on the night of June 5th:

> It is very hard to believe that in a few hours the cross Channel invasion starts! I am very uneasy about the whole operation. At best it will fall so far short of the expectation of the bulk of the people, namely all those who know nothing of its difficulties. At worst it may be the most ghastly disaster of the whole war. I wish to God it were safely over.

Brooke, as we now know, was completely wrong. But Eisenhower, in his usual modest way, had a letter ready in case everything failed. Thankfully it proved completely unnecessary.

However there were many hazards, every one of which Brooke was very aware and were not unknown to Eisenhower either.

First of all, there was the weather. This allowed for very few windows of opportunity, given the enormous numbers of troops that had to be transported across the Channel, and not by the shortest route (Dover–Calais) either. So bad was the weather on June 5th that the invasion had to be cancelled for that day: it was good luck for the Allies that June 6th was a good day to cross.

(And interestingly the Germans felt that such was the state of the weather that they regarded the entire 5th-6th period as too choppy for an invasion. When D-Day actually took place Rommel, the commander of the Wehrmacht forces in the region, was on holiday in Germany with his family.)

Where the Allies were also lucky is that another possible transport option was June 18th. Had they crossed that day they would suddenly have been hit by a mighty storm, which as it happened wrecked many of the artificial harbours that they had put in place earlier.

Second, as we have seen, the Allied landings at Anzio in January 1944 had not been an immediate success, and there was much apprehension that far worse could happen in Normandy, where far more was at stake.

Finally Field Marshal Rommel was a known factor to the British and Americans, and here again the Allies were fortunate that he had been overruled in the strategy that he wished to employ to combat landings in France. His preference was to fight on the beaches themselves, which would have made all five of the Allied landing zones ferociously contested. Thankfully Hitler had agreed instead with the other key German commander in the region, Field Marshal von Rundstedt, that Panzer divisions and similar units should be held back from the beaches themselves and a small way inland.

But it is also true to say that Allied ingenuity and creative genius made a vast difference to the success on June 6th.

One of the key problems for any amphibious operation is to have harbour facilities, and while the Allies aimed to capture actual working harbours as soon as possible there were none suitable in the landing areas. So as Paul Kennedy reminds us in *Engineers for Victory* the British came up with the brilliant idea of artificial floating harbours, nicknamed 'mulberries'. This meant that the troops could be supplied as soon as an individual mulberry was created, and so further troops and material could be sent as soon as the first wave of attackers had captured the beachheads.

Second, the British also invented special transports for tanks, which not only enabled them to land more easily but also flailed mines away. Many have argued that it was American failure to use such devices that among other things caused so many US casualties at Omaha beach. Such ingenious devices were known as 'funnies' and bore the hallmarks of the eccentric British General Percy Hobart. Churchill's encouragement both of innovation and of eccentrics paid considerable dividends on D-Day.

Churchill also once said that truth was so important that it had to be surrounded by a bodyguard of lies. British deception plans were some of the most advanced of the war, as we saw with Mincemeat, the scheme that deflected the Germans from knowing about the Allied invasion of Sicily in 1943. The British Security Service (MI5) had in fact a huge array of double agents, people whom the Germans thought were working for German intelligence but who in fact had been 'turned' and were really working for the British. Similarly the Double Cross (XX) system, led by Sir Charles Masterman, had not only recruited and used a double agent, but one who had invented scores of fictitious agents all over the country, giving the Germans the false information invented by British intelligence.

Of all the Allied plots, perhaps the most important in terms of outcome was Operation Fortitude, a massive deception plot, backed up by imaginary information from the non-existent XX agents that pretended that the Allied invasion of Europe would not be in Normandy, but in Calais. Entire fake armies were invented by the British, including one in the south of England supposedly commanded by General Patton.

In fact, Paul Kennedy reminds us, there was a northern element to Fortitude as well. As we saw, the Germans correctly guessed that Churchill would have loved to come back to Norway and reinvade the country, after the 1940 debacle. But the Chiefs of Staff wisely forbade his plan, codenamed Jupiter. However as a ruse to deceive the Germans, British intelligence encouraged the Germans to think that Churchill had got his way, and Fortitude North was a plan to make the Wehrmacht think that an invasion of Norway was imminent. Right down to 1945 the Germans kept no fewer than 400,000 troops in Norway. Their presence there was utterly useless, but 400,000 Wehrmacht soldiers thus not available to fight the Allies in Normandy.

Deception therefore worked, as did Allied technical genius, and these were two vital factors on D-Day.

Also immensely successful was the fact that it was a 'triphibious' operation, with the Air Forces of the USA and the United Kingdom along with the Royal Navy all acting in harmony with the Armed Forces. Bomber Command chafed at the idea of having to support the Army, but Eisenhower was successful in his insistence, helped by the fact that his Deputy was a Royal Air Force officer, Sir Douglas Tedder. As a result, the Luftwaffe, already seriously weakened, was able to fly only a comparatively small number of sorties, and the Allies were able to enjoy critical air superiority throughout the operation. Likewise, the Royal

Navy were untroubled by German interference, because they also succeeded in preventing damage from submarines. (Enemy 'E-boats' had inflicted hideous damage on the Allied dummy-run for D-Day at Slapton Sands in Devon on April 28th 1944, when over 900 American soldiers died.) The co-operation of all three services, Army, Navy and Air Force, contributed to making a critical difference to Allied success. The naval and air support that the Allied armies received was vital.

Critics of films such as *Saving Private Ryan* dislike the fact that Hollywood downplays the British contribution to such historic events as D-Day. However, even the British often ignore the enormous Canadian contribution. One of the five landing beaches, Juno, was Canadian, and troops from Canada made a substantial difference to the Allied war effort all the way to VE-Day.

Two of the landing beaches were British: Gold and Sword. The other two were American: Utah and Omaha. The latter, Omaha, was the only landing ground upon which all the fears and doubts came close to being realised. In reading the often very detailed accounts, one can only conclude that much of what went wrong on Omaha was as much bad luck as bad judgement. Some of the troops just landed that much too far away. Of the five beaches it was the only one that could be defended by the Germans with ease. The fact that Utah went right shows that American planning was fully up to speed.

Ten days on from D-Day half-a-million Allied soldiers and some 77,000 military vehicles had successfully been landed in France. It was a triumph of improvisation and logistics as well as of the enormous bravery of the first wave of landing troops. This includes the many parachute divisions that had landed behind enemy lines the night before, such as the famous US 82nd Airborne and the 2nd Ranger Battalion on the day itself. Death counts vary between 2,500 and around 4,400 for Allied casualties. Such a figure is happily nowhere remotely near the 57,000 killed on July 1st 1916. All deaths are tragic, but the fact that the Allies landed successfully against many odds and had comparatively so few fatalities is a huge tribute to the brave men themselves and to their leaders.

The two-front war was now fully under way. The democracies had landed and their troops were coming. The liberation of Europe had begun.

OPERATION GOODWOOD

July 18th–20th 1944

Operation Goodwood was the attempt by the British in July 1944 to capture Caen. This was an objective originally set for the first day of D-Day, but whose seizure by the Allies so early in the campaign was surely always unrealistic.

Three British armoured divisions under the overall command of General Sir Miles Dempsey were to capture a ridge to the east of the Norman town of Caen, in conjunction with a similar Canadian operation, Atlantic.

Dempsey was a great believer in the project, but new research suggests that it was his Group Commander, Monty himself, who was cautious about how many British objectives could be achieved.

Montgomery is without doubt Britain's most controversial Field Marshal and commander in World War II, mainly on account of his extraordinary arrogance to his American colleagues, who did not appreciate his constant belittling of them. One of the problems in assessing him is his own memoirs. These always give the hint that he got everything perfectly planned ahead, and that everything that happened under his command was exactly as he had predicted. He was very much a details person, and someone who could never even admit to the slightest mistake, especially if it showed him in a bad light in relation to the Americans. In the past British writers tended to support him, but now authors and experts on both sides of the Atlantic criticise him and his micromanagement. However, while there is no defence for his bombast and self-righteousness, a new trend seeks partly to re-establish him, and above all the bravery of the British and Canadian soldiers under his command.

Goodwood is a classic example of the Montgomery genre. The excellent account in Professor John Buckley's book *Monty's Men* gives a detailed portrait of an operation slowly unfolding and edging towards failure. While the British were able to make substantial gains, the Germans managed to escape in large numbers, and so one website has, with due understanding, called it a 'strategic Allied victory, a tactical German victory . . .' which about sums it up. As Professor Buckley puts it, in terms of success, Goodwood 'was both and neither . . .'

One of the real problems was that Montgomery had totally oversold the project as a major breakthrough. While the British – along with the more successful Canadians in their operation – had inflicted real damage, a transformative victory it was not. Eisenhower was apparently 'apoplectic' since he had agreed for 7,000 tons of bombs to be dropped on the

Germans. As the British gained just seven miles, Eisenhower worked out that the Allies had dropped 1,000 bombs a mile!

Churchill had also expected great things, and was disappointed, as was, more importantly by this stage, the US Army Chief of Staff, General George C. Marshall. Doubts crept in on whether or not Monty was the best person for the job of commander in the field. As usual he was protected by General Sir Alan Brooke, the Chief of the Imperial General Staff, and by his heroic status in the British popular imagination as the victor of Alamein.

However, despite Montgomery's travails, breakout was in fact imminent, as the Americans were ready . . .

OPERATION MARKET GARDEN

November 17th–25th 1944

Operation Market Garden – strictly speaking two closely linked Allied operations, Market (British) and Garden (American) – is one of the most famous of the whole war, at least so far as people in the West are concerned. It was the attempt to land on key crossings of the River Rhine, in order to be able to invade Germany proper and end the war. The capture of bridges would enable this to happen, and it is no coincidence that when the Americans actually *did* seize a vital and still intact bridge across that river in March 1945 at Remagen, then the war was over two months later.

Market Garden, while famous as one of the largest airborne/ parachute operations in history, is also infamous as one of the Western Allies' biggest failings, or so the popular version of the story goes.

The legend of Market Garden really originates with a book by the writer Cornelius Ryan, entitled *A Bridge Too Far*, and the British-directed Hollywood film of the same name. One of the major problems of film-history is that we tend to remember what we see at the cinema rather than what actually happened. This means of course that what we actually recall is the angle taken by the film producer rather than the events that took place on the ground in real life. The phrase 'a bridge too far' is attributed to General 'Boy' Browning, a key member of Montgomery's staff, to a distressed officer asking him why the operation had failed. The final bridge, at Arnhem, was according to Montgomery's words to Browning, 'a bridge too far'.

Is it all really that simple? What is so significant about the film is that the commander behind the operation – Field Marshal Sir Bernard Montgomery (as he now was) – does not appear in the film at all. Plenty of other key players do appear, especially General Sir Brian Horrocks, commander of the British XXX Corps (and played by Edward Fox), and the US airborne General James Gavin (played by Ryan O'Neal). One general Roy Urquhart failed to reach Arnhem. Sean Connery's portrayal of him is bound to influence how we see the unfolding events. Two exceptionally brave soldiers who took part in real life, the British paratrooper John Frost (played by Anthony Hopkins) and Julian Cook (played by Robert Redford), also have key roles in the film.

Market Garden was an attempt by Montgomery to be bold. Since he has normally been criticised for his excess caution, this is an unusual charge. People at the time said it was like a teetotaller becoming suddenly drunk, and Monty's sweeping plan, to cross the Rhine and then charge across northern Germany to Berlin, is usually said to be out of character. But it is important to remember that the idea was signed off by Eisenhower himself, at a rather fraught meeting between the two men in Brussels, Ike having recently injured himself and thus being in pain. This was important since the latter was now the overall field commander of the Allied armies, Montgomery having stepped down from that role earlier in the month.

One of the major problems that the Allies at this time faced was that of supply. One of the most frequent criticisms of Montgomery that is convincing is that he failed to realise the critical logistical problems that the invaders now faced. Even though Paris was back in Allied hands, they needed ports to be able to bring vitally needed supplies and spare parts from England. This was nicknamed the 'Red Ball Express' for the trucks that brought over material.

The Allies had just managed by this time to seize the key port of Antwerp, but as the Canadians discovered, the banks of the River Scheldt were under German control. Indeed it would take until November, long after Market Garden was over, to be able to utilise the port properly. Antony Beevor argues cogently that if the Canadians had been able to capture the Scheldt banks straight away, then Antwerp could have been open months earlier and without the near 13,000 Canadian casualties that resulted from the delay. It is almost certainly true as well, one could argue, that a shorter supply chain would have made a vital difference to Market Garden as well, and possibly a different outcome.

A truly enormous parachute drop – British, American and Polish paratroopers – were supposed to land, capture the key bridges and then wait for the armoured might of XXX Corps to catch up with them and cross over into Germany. That at least was the plan.

Unfortunately for the Allies, the presence in Arnhem, the third and most distant bridge, of a recuperating SS Panzer division was overlooked. In addition, one of the best German commanders, Field Marshal Model, was in the area, able to take charge swiftly once it became apparent that Allied forces were landing in numbers near him.

But perhaps the most irreconcilable problem was the major falling out between Montgomery and Eisenhower, Monty and Ike. Eisenhower, in classic American military doctrine, wanted a broad front approach to Germany, with Allied armies spread, widely backed by maximum firepower. Montgomery now decided that he wanted a single thrust approach, to smash through the Ruhr and go in one gigantic single push to Berlin.

Both plans had merits and have been argued over constantly by historians and armchair generals ever since. As Market Garden did not succeed, and as the failure to clear the Scheldt earlier led to massive Allied logistical problems, there is a sense in which the argument is futile. Once the Americans did secure a bridgehead over the Rhine in March 1945, and the British a few days later further upstream, victory came swiftly, and on Eisenhower's terms.

But one of the key issues is that back in September 1944 Montgomery naturally wanted to command the sharp dagger thrust himself. He was by now completely *persona non grata* not only to many of the most important American commanders in the field, including Eisenhower's deputy Air Chief Marshal Tedder, but also to several of the British commanders.

Consequently, when the great campaign to capture the bridges was launched on September 17th, things were not as they should be.

Although the famous film does portray Julian Cook's astonishingly brave crossing of the River Waal, and the American capture of the bridge intact, according to plan, it does not make clear that one entire half of the plan – Market – was a complete success. The US forces captured all their target bridges, just as Montgomery had planned. But it is fair to point out that neither the British nor the Americans had in their original plans capturing *both* sides of each bridge. Had this been planned the situation at Arnhem would have been very different for Frost and his brave paratroopers, and Cook would never have had to cross the River Waal in daylight and under heavy enemy fire.

The problem therefore was in the Garden part of the operation, and in the attempt by British/Polish forces to seize the final bridge, at Arnhem.

With the Arnhem operation, everything possible went wrong. The troops were landed eight miles away and many of the radios simply failed to work.

Here one sees how reality and films can differ. Everyone knew ahead of time that the British would land that far away from the target, including General Urquhart himself. More important still, Browning – unlike the character played as a villain by Dirk Bogarde – knew, as did everyone else involved in the planning, about the existence of Panzer divisions nearby. Along with Montgomery, one of the other key players in Market Garden is not portrayed in the film, namely General Sir Miles Dempsey, the British army commander in overall charge of

XXX Corps. (The actual commander of XXX, General Sir Brian Horrocks, is in the film, played by Edward Fox.) Dempsey felt that Arnhem was a mistake, and that Wesel would be a much more important town to capture. And it seems that other leading British commanders did too, such as General David Belchem, who was on Montgomery's staff. Even Browning had his doubts. But as Montgomery was in charge, Arnhem was selected and the others then followed his orders.

Significantly Dempsey had doubts about Urquhart. This was not connected to his bravery, which was not in question, but to his experience, which was slender. Since the character in the film is played by Sean Connery, a naturally sympathetic actor, we see Urquhart in the light of James Bond, rather than as the enthusiastic but out-of-depth person that he might well have been in real life. And Browning was certainly not as portrayed by Bogarde, and the failure at Arnhem was in real life to end Browning's command in the field.

Recent thinking on Arnhem suggests that even thinking of getting as far as that bridge was flawed. The Americans felt at the time that XXX Corps, and in particular the tank crews of the (British) Guards Armoured Division – the Michael Caine composite in the film – lacked martial vigour. They were horrified when British troops stopped to have tea!

But in fact to get sixty miles down heavily contested territory, which is what Montgomery's plan asked XXX and the American 82nd Airborne Division to achieve, was always, it is now felt, an impossible task. This would have been the case without any tea breaks or with the British breaking normal rules and driving tanks through the night as well as in daytime.

In addition, even the Americans found themselves snarled and slowed by the sheer force of the German opposition. New writing on Arnhem thinks that there was an element of hubris in the Allied belief that victory was achievable from the West and by Christmas. The fact that the Panzer divisions were known about and discounted is given in evidence of this, and it is a strong case.

Consequently, the fact that the Allies were able to get two of the key bridges – Eindhoven and Nijmegen – can be seen as a major achievement. The failure of the ground forces to reach as far as Arnhem, while tragic for those British troops captured, injured or killed, is understandable as the force of German opposition would always have been too powerful to overcome.

Montgomery, therefore, rather than British tea breaks, was responsible for what went wrong. As now seems apparent, airborne operations were always highly risky, and the experience of the forces under Urquhart at Arnhem was by no means unique. To take another and more recent portrayal of the war, *Band of Brothers*, for parachute divisions to be dropped a long way from the correct target was a natural hazard of war. The argument goes, landing far away was if anything more normal than to arrive at the exact target.

So Montgomery's plan had at least three major flaws:

An over-reliance on paratroopers landing in the right spot.

The idea that only one side of a bridge needed to be captured.

The notion that ground troops could cover all the area necessary within the relevant time needed to catch up with the airborne troops at their respective bridges.

Only one of these ideas needed to go wrong for the operation to fail, and one could argue that in fact all three went seriously astray. XXX Corps had to cover and capture no less than sixty miles. Goodwood had shown how hard it was even to succeed in venturing seven miles, let alone sixty.

Therefore, with the failure of Market Garden, and the potentially even greater error in postponing the capture and opening of the Scheldt until late November, the Allied effort in north-west Europe was stalled. There would be no victory by Christmas.

How much difference did the debacle at Arnhem make to the outcome of the war? Could the Western Allies have made it to Berlin, as many had hoped?

There is, as is so often the case in the history of the Second World War, more than one opinion. Take the two below, which differ completely from one another, and decide accordingly.

The first is from the British book *Monty's Men*, which argues that

Perhaps the greatest tragedy was that even if Arnhem had been reached in time and the bridges secured, this would anyway not have resulted in the collapse of German resistance and brought an end to the war. Far from being on the point of surrender, German strength was recovering, while the stretched supply lines of the Allies were continuing to hinder their operations and would in any case soon have curtailed Montgomery's dream of speeding on to Berlin.

By contrast, the American author Mitchell Bard, in *The Complete Idiot's Guide to World War II* (second edition, 2004) writes:

> If Operation Market Garden had succeeded, the Allies would probably have reached Berlin weeks before the Russians, ending the war by Christmas 1944, saved thousands of civilian and military lives, and perhaps changed the fate of postwar Europe. Instead it took another four months before the Allies crossed the Rhine and began the final conquest of Germany.

Either way, though, Hitler's last throw made a critical difference. On December 16th 1944, as we shall see, the Germans launched what has become known as the 'Battle of the Bulge'. The war in the West was about to get complicated.

THE BATTLE OF THE BULGE

December 16th 1944–January 25th 1945

Original hopes that the Allies could get to Berlin by Christmas 1944 had been dashed by logistical difficulties and the failure to capture enough bridges across the River Rhine to expedite a major Allied offensive into Germany.

In fact, on December 16th, it would not be a Western Allied attack that would set the pace but a German counter-attack, known to the Wehrmacht as Operation Watch on the Rhine, or Autumn Mist, and to people in Allied nations as the Battle of the Bulge. The name comes from the fact that the Americans were in a large bulge or salient, in the Ardennes area of Belgium, France and Luxembourg.

The attack had not really been expected. Indeed the German generals in charge of it were not wild about it either, including the notional commander, Field Marshal Rundstedt. This was very much Hitler's plan, an attack on Antwerp that would also cut off the Canadian armies and perhaps cause Canada and the USA to leave the war. This attack, along with the secret rockets (the V1 and V2), was, Hitler thought, a way to win the war.

All this was pure fantasy, as his commanders knew. It was very much a gambler's last throw of the dice, but in reality it was also Hitler's absolute last chance of a counter-offensive, since if it failed, all was lost.

The attack started on December 16th and took the Americans completely by surprise. Hodges, in charge of the First Army, had a breakdown, and the power of the German bombardment also had the effect of severing much of the American communication system, isolating commands from each other.

The news got to Eisenhower on what was supposed to be a day of rest. Thankfully his guest that day was General Bradley, and the two senior US commanders were able to find out a great deal of what was happening, amidst the fog of uncertainty, and to plot accordingly. Since US troops had been cut off, it made sense to Eisenhower to make the relief operation something under Montgomery's command. Bradley was enraged by this, since, as the Americans expected, Monty was swiftly to use his new enhanced position to rubbish US tactics – in what Antony Beevor, in his wonderful detailed description of the unfolding drama calls the 'Battle of Montgomery's ego'.

Fortunately for everyone the other supreme egoist, Patton, was not placed under Monty's command. His Third Army launched into the fray, to Patton's joy, but with just three divisions it was not able to accomplish all that its leader wished. Bradley was also able to redeploy many US forces, coming at the Germans from the south, and Horrocks achieved the same for the British XXX Corps, en route from the north.

For Americans, the enormous bravery and sheer courage of both the encircled soldiers and of those coming to the rescue has made the battle one of the iconic struggles of the whole Second World War. It was not at all easy for those parachute regiments flown in to relieve beleaguered troops. Many of them were still in summer uniforms, in what were now appalling winter conditions, and trench foot in foxholes became a major health hazard. Nonetheless units such as the 82nd and 101st Airborne reinforced not only the surrounded forces but also their heroic status.

In particular the siege of the town of Bastogne has become legendary in the USA. At a time of serious crisis in his own Presidency, John F Kennedy (himself a veteran of the war in the Pacific) raised the memory of the successful US defence of Bastogne as a means of encouraging the American people.

Also part of US folklore was the characteristic reply of Brigadier Anthony McAuliffe, who was told by the Germans to surrender Bastogne. His demotic reply of 'nuts' is famous as the embodiment of American pluck and determination in the face of adversity.

Bastogne held out and survived. Montgomery had been requested to launch a major Allied counter-offensive, and this finally took place on January 3rd. This was some while after the Americans had wanted but, typical of cautious Montgomery, only when he felt certain that everything was ready to go.

Success was swift. While the USA had 9,000 casualties and no fewer than 15,000 taken prisoner, their Allied colleagues under Montgomery were swiftly able to crush the German forces. The latter lost 80 to 100,000 men, some 1,000 Luftwaffe planes and no less than 800 tanks. Since German supplies were already at an absolute nadir, these losses were catastrophic for a Reich now firmly on its last legs.

Antony Beevor has aptly called this Eisenhower's finest hour. His adaptability, his calmness and his firm resolution all came through, and the crisis shows him at his very best. While it might be fashionable to decry American leadership in Europe, the story of the Battle of the Bulge shows that this is unfair, since Bradley and Patton also came out of it well. Montgomery ended the siege, but his boasting of his successes and his vainglorious verbal attacks on his American colleagues further worsened the already strained inter-Allied relationships. Brooke in London and Montgomery's chief aide de Guigand in the field had to spend much time in damage limitation whenever Montgomery spoke.

PART FIVE: II

1944

The Eastern Front

OPERATION BAGRATION

June 22nd–August 19th 1944

Operation Bagration was one of the biggest military encounters in history, in keeping with the epic scale of the battles of the Eastern Front in World War II. Intended for June 19th 1944, it was finally launched three days later, auspiciously on the third anniversary of Barbarossa in 1941. But this time it was the Soviets who were on the offensive.

Historians as well as people at the time have thought that it was launched in order to help the Allies on D-Day, which had begun on June 6th. Not everyone is now sure of this, even though the great Marshal Zhukov stated it as such in his memoirs. It could be that Stalin thought it an opportune moment to wipe out the German Army Group Centre, something that he had been contemplating back that April.

Either way, the operation, named after Prince Peter (Pyotr) Bagration, an heroic Russian general of Georgian origin – not therefore unlike Stalin himself – was unleashed just over two weeks after D-Day.

We saw that ten days after D-Day that the Western Allies had around 500,000 troops in Normandy. Figures for the number of Soviet forces seem to differ substantially, many giving around 1.8 million, or over three times as many Red Army troops for this operation as Allied in France. But other and perhaps more reliable sources give the grand total for the Red Army for Bagration as a staggering 2.4 million, which is almost five times the number of Soviet forces now facing the Germans as the Allies on June 16th. The new and probably accurate guesstimate gives the Soviets 2.4 million troops, 5,200 tanks and self-propelled guns, and some 5,300 combat aircraft. By any account, this amount is gigantic in scale and dwarfs anything seen in the West.

Some indication of the German deployments is salutary. Just before D-Day there were 60 German divisions in France, 27 in Italy and no fewer than 156 on the Eastern Front. In the enormous clash that was now to take place in Belarus/Central Russia, the German commander Field Marshal Ernst Busch possessed approximately 800,000 men or fifty-one divisions, only a tiny amount smaller than the German divisions that faced the Allies in Normandy on D-Day.

Yet a single instance of how much we fail to take the Eastern Front seriously: everyone in the West has heard of D-Day, and (to be fair to Westerners) of some battles such as Stalingrad. But Bagration is not so well known in the West, even though it was to destroy far more German forces than on D-Day and to do so in much faster time.

There were four large Army Groups on the Soviet side – the First, Second and Third Belorussian Armies and the First Baltic Army. The two northern fronts were under the overall strategic command of Marshal Zhukov, and the two southern army groups under that of Marshal Vassilevsky. Significantly, much of the Soviet armour was of American make, through Lend-Lease. Although Stalin wanted everyone to know how the Soviet peoples were suffering uniquely in the struggle against fascism, he and subsequent Soviet accounts of these battles tend to downplay the massive contribution in material terms by the capitalist USA.

The Soviet forces were using the so-called 'deep battle' techniques that had been pioneered in the USSR in the 1930s, but by officers who had been shot on Stalin's orders in the Great Purge from 1937 onwards. But needs must, and in the same way that Stalin was happy to rehabilitate the Russian Orthodox Church for patriotic purposes, so too did the 'deep battle' technique of the now purged come to the rescue in order successfully to beat the Germans.

In the West we are very aware of *blitzkrieg*, of the German Panzer tanks racing through countries and conquering them as if in an afternoon. By 1943 it was in fact obvious that while such doctrine could be applied in Western countries with modern roads and railways, the USSR was a very different place. The Germans had been very influenced by a Briton, Sir Basil Liddell Hart, who regarded Panzer Generals such as Guderian as among his best pupils. Because of the respect shown to a British thinker by the Wehrmacht, we tend, wrongly perhaps, to be in unique awe of German military prowess and doctrine.

John Buckley and a new generation of historians have shown, in books such as *Monty's Men*, that this semi-worship of German genius and military might is seriously overplayed. But if it was true that the brave British and American troops on D-Day were better than has been thought, how much more true is the futility of German technique and fighting prowess on the Eastern Front? The German Central Front was now smashed beyond repair by the Soviets, with the latter using the military doctrine of 'deep battle' that was wholly Russian in origin.

It has best been described by Soviet history specialist Evan Mawdsley as follows:

> The theoretical essence of deep battle was to attack the enemy using very fast-moving mechanised troops, air strikes and parachute landings. Simultaneous blows were to be struck through the depth of the enemy's defensive system.

The importance of this cannot be exaggerated. Significantly, during the Cold War, when the USSR replaced Nazi Germany as the enemy of freedom, NATO commanders and military analysts were to study deep battle in depth. Now this strategy has migrated across the Atlantic, since a twenty-first-century version of it is the kind of 'shock and awe' approach used by the USA.

Whether or not the more modern American version worked is outside the scope of this book, and is of course profoundly controversial! But it is interesting that commanders from Marshal

Zhukov in the 1940s to General Colin Powell in recent times all bear the influence of purged Russian military strategists in the 1930s.

What is apparent with Bagration is that the *kessel*, or enveloping manoeuvre, used with such effect by the Germans in 1941, was now being used against them by their former victims, the Red Army. Hitler had ordered various towns in Belarus to be like fortifications, but the four in the path of the Soviet juggernaut (Vitebsk, Orsha, Mogilev and Bobruisk – places known by different names at other times) were surrounded and captured just as so many Ukrainian and Russian cities had been three years earlier.

On July 3rd the Belarus capital, Minsk, was retaken, almost effortlessly. Within just two weeks of the launch of Bagration some seventy per cent of all the Army Group Centre forces had been wiped out. The shattered remnants of the German armies were pushed back no less than 300 miles. The Red Army had forced them to retreat so far that they ended up just sixty miles away from Hitler's Wolf's Lair headquarters in East Prussia.

The damage done to the Germans had been overwhelming. As ever, exact numbers are hard to come by and are the source of ongoing debate and controversy. But everyone agrees that the Germans fatalities were far greater during Bagration even than in the charnel house of Stalingrad. But in the more successful struggle in June–August 1944, with the First Belorussian Army Group reaching the Vistula on August 1st, the Red Army had won one of the most significant and successful military campaigns in history.

The Allies in Normandy were operating at a comparative

snail's pace, despite Patton's efforts to instil some martial vigour. But the losses to the Red Army victors in Bagration were on an even more devastating scale than anything in France. In fact one study of the 1941–1945 Eastern Front reckons that the Soviets lost in almost all three-month periods *more* than the entire amount of men lost by the USA. *Total* American losses for the entire war in all theatres, Pacific as well as European, were some 300,000. In Bagration alone the Soviets lost some 180,000 men, six times as many as the US losses in Normandy over the identical period.

But it was the German losses of approximately 590,000 on the entire Eastern Front in that time frame (June–August 1944) that was to be truly catastrophic. Thousands of German prisoners of war were paraded through the streets of Moscow in a celebration reminiscent of Roman triumphs in ancient times. These were people whom the Third Reich simply could not replace, and as we have seen replacement is one of the most important factors in winning or losing a war. The Red Army could always replenish lost lives; the Wehrmacht could not.

THE WARSAW UPRISING

August 1st–October 2nd 1944

One thing that has puzzled many readers of Winston Churchill's magisterial war memoirs, *The History of the Second World War*, is the title of the sixth and final volume, *Triumph and Tragedy*. Triumph we all understand! VE-Day and then VJ-Day, both in 1945, were major victories. They marked the end of years of global war in which tens of millions had died, but at the end of which Germany and Japan were comprehensively defeated. So what was the tragedy?

It was the issue of Poland. Britain had gone to war in September 1939 notionally to defend Poland, but now, with victory in sight by the end of 1943, the plight of Poland was to Churchill a source of permanent and grave anxiety. And he was right to be so concerned. As we saw, under the Molotov–Ribbentrop Pact of

August 1939 Poland was divided between the two tyrannies of Nazi Germany and the Soviet Union. Poland had only just come back into existence in 1918 after well over a century's foreign rule, and thus by 1939, when it was re-divided, it had again been abolished by hostile neighbours.

Stalin had never forgotten his humiliation by the Poles in the war in 1918–1920 that recreated the Polish state, much of it at the expense of the former Tsarist Empire. Tens of thousands of innocent Poles were massacred or exiled during 1939–1941. Now in July 1941 the Red Army stood again on the Vistula, ostensibly as Poland's liberator from Nazi rule. But what in fact was the truth?

One of the most important Allied conferences during the whole war took place in the Iranian capital of Tehran during November 28th–December 1st 1943. Stalin, Roosevelt and Churchill were all there. And as the last of the supposed 'Big Three' found to his cost at that meeting, it was really the Big Two and a Half. Churchill was no longer so important. The two major players were the USA and the USSR, and as we know, from 1945 until the implosion of the Soviet Union in 1991, these were to be the two 'superpowers' of the Cold War era.

Roosevelt was very concerned about Poland as well. There were lots of ancestrally ethnic Poles in the USA, as many as possible of whose votes he wanted in the Presidential Election due in November 1944. But he also wanted the USSR to be part of his peaceful new post-war order, part from the start of the projected United Nations, that came into being, after his death, in 1946.

Some have accused Roosevelt of appeasing Stalin. But it is

also possible to see him as a realist, adapting his policies to what was actually happening on the ground. We know now that when Harry Truman became President after Roosevelt's death in 1945 that he took a very different line, and kept the American troops in Europe, where they have been ever since. In 1918 though, the Americans had come home from Europe, and that is what Roosevelt also expected to happen.

But Roosevelt thought above all of Japan. Again, with hindsight, we are aware of the overwhelming results of the two atom bombs that effectively ended the war in the Pacific and caused Japan to surrender. At the time, however, in November 1943, the effects of the Manhattan Project, of the American atomic weapons development, were unknown. What the US expected then was a ground invasion of Japan, which would involve well over a million US soldiers, and possibly have casualties like no other conflict in history. This expectation was based on losses in the Pacific war so far, especially on the US Marine death toll for some of the smaller islands in the Pacific. The struggle for the Japanese main island was expected to cost hundreds of thousands of American lives.

In November 1943 the USSR and Japan were neutral in relation to each other. It was clear that Stalin would not break that neutrality until after Germany had been conquered, and for all the Allies knew then, that could be a long time into the future. Remember too that D-Day had not happened, and that there were many who presumed, like Field Marshal Sir Alan Brooke, that even that would see a bloodbath on the scale of the dead of the Somme in 1916.

So along with Soviet support for the projected United

Nations, Roosevelt was desperate to get Stalin to sign up for full-scale war with Japan once Germany had been crushed. And as it happens, although Stalin frequently lied to his Allies during the war and broke countless promises, this was not among them: after VE-Day the USSR duly broke its neutrality pact and declared war on Japan. In the end it was Hiroshima and Nagasaki that ended the war with Japan, not the Soviet intervention, but there was no way in which Roosevelt could have been aware of that back in 1943.

So Churchill was deeply concerned for Poland, and Roosevelt understood that, but the realities of war led the President to have other priorities. Remember too that in November 1943 D-Day was seven months into the future, and that millions of Soviet troops were dying in the titanic struggle on the Eastern Front.

Stalin wanted a Poland that was completely under his own control. He had a group of tame Poles, of Communists politically utterly loyal to him, in the town of Lublin, when the Red Army finally liberated that city. Even as early as December 1941, with the Germans almost in the suburbs of Moscow, Stalin had insisted to British visitors that he wanted his new 1939 borders, the fruit of his pact with Hitler, and that was that. This included all of pre-August 1939 Poland that he had annexed in collaboration with the Germans.

Ethnically speaking, much of eastern Poland was not actually Polish. Much of it had very tragically been Jewish, and millions of them were to be exterminated by the Nazis. Others were what we would now call Ukrainians or Belorussians, since Stalin was, by right of conquest, to get his way.

Not surprisingly, however, the Polish exiles based in London but fighting bravely with the Western Allies, wanted all of their country back. They knew how many Poles had been massacred by the NKVD in 1939–1941. They were more than aware that the NKVD – sometimes the same people – were in the rearguard of the Red Army, arresting thousands of people who were deemed anti-Communist in all territories liberated from the Germans.

So in late July 1944, the brave Polish Home Army, the core of the resistance to Hitler and German occupation, made the intrepid and tragically foolhardy decision to launch an uprising against the Germans in the Polish capital of Warsaw.

Foolish because although the Red Army now stood just on the other side of the Vistula, their orders were to stop for a rest break. Not only that but the Western Allies were completely forbidden by Stalin to use Soviet-held territory to give military equipment and other forms of aid to the Polish rebels.

As a consequence the gallant Poles were very much on their own. Only a tiny amount of Western aid got through as the Allied aircraft had to come from hundreds of miles away and the logistics were well nigh impossible.

Himmler ordered some of the most bloodthirsty imaginable SS divisions to suppress the uprising. The Kaminski Brigade had been formed out of the 15th SS Cossack Cavalry Corps. One of the SS officers involved organised the massacre of the rebels as he perched a monkey on his shoulder. As Antony Beevor describes it in his harrowing account of the slaughter, the SS 'appeared to enjoy their work. The wounded in Polish field hospitals were burnt alive with flamethrowers. Children were massacred for fun. Home Army nurses were whipped, raped and then murdered . . .'

All in all some 200,000 innocent Poles, a very large percentage of which were civilians, were put to death in an orgy of killing and destruction by a gleeful SS.

And the Soviets did virtually nothing to stop any of this.

Needless to say, Stalin's decision not to stop the mass-murder of hundreds of thousands of Polish people brought back to Poland the bitter memories of 1939–1941. We now know more of these atrocities than we did before through the television documentaries and books of Laurence Rees, for instance, or Norman Davies' book *Uprising '44.*

Stalin always insisted that the halt by the Red Army was for entirely military and logistical purposes. But after the triumphs of Soviet armour in brilliant campaigns such as Bagration, which represented an advance of over 300 miles, the Soviet dictator's excuse does seem very strange. Parts of the Red Army were as close as eighty miles from the outskirts of Berlin. When the great final offensive began some six months or so later, victorious Red Army troops went all the way to the German capital.

Warsaw was thus not 'liberated', if that can be the right word to use, until January 1945. To this day Polish people feel understandably bitter about what happened. As always Stalin has his apologists, not all of them ideologically Marxist or Russian nationalist, who believe his claim that the reason for the Soviet halt really was entirely strategic/logistic in nature. But the massacre of 200,000 patriotic Poles, none of whom would have supported the oppressive Soviet-supported regime that ruled Poland on Moscow's behalf until 1989, does still leave a very bitter taste in the mouth.

PART FIVE: III

1944

The War Against Japan

KOHIMA AND THE BATTLE
OF THE TENNIS COURT

April 4th–June 22nd 1944

Only the British could possibly have a Battle of the Tennis Court, but such an encounter took place in the siege of the border town of Kohima in the spring of 1944.

The Japanese occupation of Burma, which had begun early in 1942, has been described as the one place where their ground strategy worked. In essence they captured places capable of active defence, and simply held onto them, resistant to all British attempts to drive them out.

Then in 1944 General Renya Mutaguchi, in charge of the Japanese 15th Army, decided that he was the man to be able to extend the war into India, and maybe blast his way to New Delhi, the capital of the British Raj. In this he was much encouraged by rebel Indian soldiers who had switched sides and enlisted with the Japanese, on the basis of my enemy's enemy is my friend. So instead of staying put, the Japanese launched a major assault, codenamed U-GO.

However the Raj's 14th Army under General William 'Bill' Slim was perhaps the best in the British Empire. Significant too is the fact that three-quarters of his troops were Indian, and utterly loyal to their imperial overlords.

Consequently U-GO ran into trouble. In addition, the British were able to get considerable logistical support from the USA, despite the fact that the Americans regarded this whole area as a backwater of the war. (In fact the poor British soldiers in the 14th Army were to call themselves the 'forgotten army', which in comparison with, say, the more famous 8th Army under Montgomery is probably true.)

Slim's counter-offensive worked. Not only that but the fighting spirit of the British in besieged Kohima had been strengthened immeasurably by knowledge of Japanese barbarities. The latter had taken Allied prisoners and simply bayoneted them to death. So when the savage battle for an actual tennis court in Kohima ensued, the commander of one of the British regiments told his men that the Japanese 'had renounced any right to be regarded as human . . . Our backs were to the wall, and we were going to sell our lives as expensively as we could.'

Many of the Japanese attacked so vigorously because they were starving: Japanese soldiers in the field were told to live off the land. In some parts of the war, including in areas in which they were fighting Australian soldiers, Japanese troops actually resorted to cannibalism, albeit if possible of soldiers and local people who were already dead. Allied soldiers fighting Japanese troops had thus even more reason to fight on. Therefore so far as Western soldiers were concerned (Britain, its Empire, the USA), the war in the Pacific came to have an extra and vicious fighting edge that was absent from the conflict against the Italians and Germans in Europe.

Thankfully the 14th Army rescued the besieged British and Indian forces in Kohima and U-GO was smashed. Victory in Burma would take a while but Slim's forces were on their way.

THE BATTLE OF SAIPAN AND THE GREAT MARIANAS TURKEY SHOOT

June 15th–July 9th 1944

The true horrors of the Pacific War can be seen in the Battle of Saipan, one of the two major islands in the Marianas chain. This battle also demonstrates the radically different attitude to life held by two distinct cultures: Japan and the West.

On June 15th, 20,000 US forces landed on the island of Saipan (with a further 40,000 following close behind). Once again the Japanese defenders fought with total fanaticism and this time there were no fewer than 32,000 of them, all prepared to die for their cause. The US Navy bombardment did not manage to destroy the bunkers, so the invading Marines had to fight all the way.

It took three weeks just to subdue the island. The Japanese commander committed suicide, and, in effect, so did 3,000 to

4,000 of his troops. They staged a 'banzai' attack on July 7th at oncoming American fire that killed nearly all of the Japanese forces.

There were no fewer than 14,000 US killed and wounded (nearly 4,000 killed) and well over 30,000 Japanese soldiers died in their defence of Saipan. But what makes this battle truly grisly is the 7,000 Japanese civilian suicides, all people who ended their lives by jumping from cliffs into the sea below.

Thankfully for the USA, but again to the loss of the Japanese, the naval battle fought simultaneously proved to be an overwhelming American success and with far fewer Allied casualties. Officially this is the Battle of the Philippine Sea, but because of the superb prowess of the US Navy planes it has gone down in folklore as the 'Great Marianas Turkey Shoot'.

Here, as historians have pointed out, US technology prevailed. There was a new kind of fighter, the appropriately named 'Hellcat'. In addition, in the naval engagement, there were fifteen American carriers and just nine Japanese. In the battle itself the USA lost 29 fighters, the Japanese 243, a huge discrepancy. Three of the Japanese carriers were sunk, and two further were damaged. The industrial might of the USA was now beginning to tell.

We have seen in an earlier chapter that Roosevelt was consulting around this time at Pearl Harbor with Nimitz and MacArthur, to the latter's advantage. But we also ought to look at how American thinking was developing.

The Americans were weighing up in their minds how many lives a US-led invasion of the Japanese home island would cost. If the Japanese fought as fanatically as they did on Saipan, the answer could be in terms of hundreds of thousands of American deaths and injuries. Furthermore the Japanese civilian populations had been indoctrinated not just with blind fanaticism and obedience to the Emperor-cult but also with terror of what the Westerners might inflict upon them.

The Manhattan Project, the US project to build the atomic bomb, begins to figure in the thinking of strategists in high places. It would provide an alternative, albeit horrible, to all the suicides and an even more terrible death toll on the mainland.

We know of course that when the Americans landed in Japan after VJ-Day that they treated their former enemies with utmost decorum. But so isolated culturally and psychologically were the Japanese in the homeland that they did not understand this. If 7,000 Japanese civilians could commit suicide in Saipan, despite endless requests from the Americans to surrender peacefully and safely, what worse horrors might follow if the Allies landed on the sacred soil of Japan itself?

We are rightly horrified by the spectre of what happened at Hiroshima and Nagasaki, and by the existential terror faced by millions during the Cold War of the total destruction of all humanity if a nuclear World War III had ever occurred. But in 1944 this was all ahead of everyone aiming to make the decision on what to do with Japan, and on how to end the war. Max Hastings is surely right to pose this question in the many books he has written on World War II in general, and on the war in the Pacific in particular. We have to forget what we now know, and try to see how they saw things at the time. The horrors of Saipan repeated on an altogether larger scale in Japan itself would have dwarfed the death toll in Hiroshima and Nagasaki. And being responsible to their own men, and aware of what Japanese civilians could do to themselves, the America planners' train of thought is thus easier to see.

Saipan also altered the Japanese conduct of the war. Admiral Tojo, who had led the government since 1941, resigned following the loss of the island. The new administration seemed as fanatical as ever, but slowly it dawned on some people in Japan that the war could no longer be won, and that a way out might now need to be sought.

THE BATTLE OF LEYTE GULF

October 23rd–26th 1944

The Battle of Leyte Gulf, fought in the Philippines between the Japanese Imperial Navy and the US Navy, is a contender for the title of largest naval engagement in the Second World War. Some have gone so far as to claim for it the status of the biggest naval battle in history, a description that it might well deserve.

It was assuredly the largest naval task force that the US has assembled. There were over 700 American ships. Admiral Halsey's own section of it, the Third Fleet, contained eighteen carriers, six battleships, sixty-four destroyers and seventeen cruisers.

Naval battles are very complex manoeuvres to depict in short spaces. Suffice it to say here that initially the battle went Halsey's way, and that the Japanese fleet had to make two withdrawals in order to survive. By the time of the Japanese retreat, the Imperial

Navy had lost thirty-six ships in total, including ten destroyers and six heavy cruisers and four carriers.

But on October 25th the Japanese launched the weapon that showed how completely desperate they had become: *kamikaze* pilots flying straight into ships. The death of the pilot was guaranteed, but so too, if the plane reached its target, was the sinking of the ship.

Kamikaze means 'divine wind', a reference to a gigantic storm at sea that destroyed a Mongol invasion fleet heading towards Japan some centuries before. Now the Japanese thought that self-sacrifice – as the pilot always died – would end the American invasion, which was becoming ever more certain.

On the first day of the *kamikaze* strikes, the US fleet lost thirty-three of its ships, for the loss of no less than 5,000 suicide *kamikaze* pilots. This was a particularly hideous form of warfare, one utterly alien to the Western mind. Its horror created a visceral feeling towards the perpetrators that left deep scars in the thoughts and attitudes of the Americans. It might, in the long term, have been subconsciously part of the rationale for the atom bomb drops on Japan in 1945. If the Japanese were *that* fanatical, then only something truly massive – such as an atom bomb – would induce them to surrender.

Halsey, whose nickname was 'Bull', had let some of the Japanese fleet go before destroying most of the rest. His decision has been attributed to communications failure. But even though his action has thus also been nicknamed, as 'Bull's Run', it is probably fair to say that so much of the Japanese fleet had been destroyed that it was now effectively worthless against American progress towards the goal of defeating Japan.

PART SIX: I

1945

The Eastern Front

THE RED ARMY
VISTULA–ODER OFFENSIVE

January12th–February 9th 1945

In January 1945 Marshal Zhukov, the great Soviet commander, was put in charge of the 1st Belorussian Army Group. His colleague Marshal Konev commanded the 1st Ukrainian Army Group, and in addition there was a 2nd Belorussian Army Group. Between these three vast formations, each of which had several armies, there were substantially over 2,000,000 Red Army soldiers ready for the final assault on the Third Reich. Two of these Army Groups, Zhukov's and Konev's, were at the core of the Vistula–Oder offensive.

Zhukov indeed thought that the war would be over by February, and there is little question that had his group, the 1st Belorussian, been allowed to smash through to the German capital straight away, that he could have achieved such a goal. The cost in Soviet lives would have been huge, but since that proved to be the case anyway, one could argue that it might actually have saved lives. If Germany had been defeated by February, which Zhukov's plan would have made entirely feasible, then not only would hundreds of thousands of Red Army lives have been saved but also those among the Western Allies who died fighting in the period February–May 1945.

(In the battle of memoirs, Zhukov defended the decision to halt while Marshal Chuikov argued that the Red Army should have continued. But at the time the plan to make straight for Berlin was Zhukov's.)

Marshal Konev was also a keen supporter of continuing to Berlin.

Now that we know more about what the Soviets were doing and thinking, it should be possible to understand why the huge Red Army juggernaut set in motion on January 12th, with perhaps as many as 2,300,000 soldiers and well over 4,000 tanks, all suddenly came to a stop. To say that it was 'successful' as online sources state without qualification is to avoid the question: why did it stop?

It ended at roughly the same time as the Yalta Conference in the Crimea, February 7th–11th 1945. This was the last meeting of the 'Big Three' since Roosevelt died in April and Churchill lost power in the 1945 General Election (strictly speaking two months after it, but it took two months to count the votes from servicemen overseas). By this time Stalin was in charge of much of Eastern Europe, and as historian John Grigg once suggested, what Stalin took he kept. Whatever Churchill's concerns about the fate of the Poles, since Poland had been conquered by the Red

Army, Stalin decreed it would remain under Communist rule whatever the West might think.

But while the archives of the USSR tell us much, they still do not explain why Stalin diverted his armies in February 1945 and effectively delayed the final assault on Berlin. This is especially strange since by January 31st they were a mere forty-three miles from the German capital, and could easily have continued. (Konev's armies were not that far away either.)

Many theories exist.

What in effect now happened is that the Red Army spent two months attacking towards its flanks, one to the south, to the area of Germany then called Silesia, and the other to a part of Germany then known as Pomerania. Significantly both these regions, historically and ethnically German for centuries, are now part of Poland. Each was a former part of Germany granted to the Poles by the victorious Red Army in 1945, in recompense for the huge eastern areas of Poland annexed by the USSR first in 1939 and then again in 1945 (and now parts of Belarus and Ukraine respectively).

It could be that Stalin wanted to ensure the conquest of areas that he intended to carve up once victory was won. Hundreds of thousands of both Red Army troops and Wehrmacht soldiers died, for instance, to seize the historic Prussian city of Königsberg. This is now the Russian city of Kaliningrad, that strange enclave of the Russian Federation on the Baltic Sea, now detached from the rest of its mother country by Polish territory. Stalin was determined to annexe these areas to the USSR, and their conquest by Red Army forces certainly allowed this to take place, as Stalin hoped.

It is also thought that the Soviet dictator had nightmares

about the time in 1918–1920 when the Red Army looked as if it were about to capture Warsaw, and then proceeded to invade the West. Stalin was a Commissar at that time, and remembered bitterly how the invaders were hit hard on their two flanks, such that their impetus was lost. He might therefore have feared that to go straight for Berlin without safeguarding both Pomerania and Silesia could lead to a major military setback for the USSR. Better to be sure, and take two or three extra months, this theory goes, than aim straight for Berlin only to be cut off by Wehrmacht soldiers still holding out to the north and south of the Red Army.

This theory for what has been called the 'Halt on the Oder' certainly makes sense. Remember too that at that particular point, the Western forces had yet to cross the Rhine. Stalin felt that he had time on his hands.

Hundreds of thousands of both Red Army troops and also Wehrmacht soldiers would die in these two new flanking manoeuvres. In the south, one of the main Silesian cities, Breslau (now the Polish town of Wroclaw) would hold out until May. The same was true of the hundreds of thousands of German troops in what was then called Courland, another region where Germans have lived for centuries but which after 1945 was to be carved up by Stalin in his redrawing of the map of Europe.

So the conquest of Berlin was delayed.

But then Stalin heard about the crossing of the River Rhine at Remagen in March, by the Americans. Come the beginning of April, the race for Berlin resumed. The end of the war in Europe was now in sight.

THE BATTLES FOR CENTRAL EUROPE

February 13th–May 11th 1945

As experts on southern Central European history of this period remind us, we concentrate either on the attack on Germany from the West (if we are Western) or from the East (if we are Russian or Polish). We forget that great battles were fought between the Germans and the Red Army over much of southern Central Europe as well; countries such as Hungary, what was then Czechoslovakia and what became Austria again in 1945. And notice the unusual final date – May 11th, three days after VE-Day and the formal surrender of the Third Reich.

In 1944 the Romanians, realising that the situation for them as a Nazi ally was hopeless, surrendered via their King, Michael, a cousin of the British Royal Family. In the long term this was to make no difference to Romania's fate, since that nation soon became an Iron Curtain satellite state of the USSR until 1989.

In the short term it did mean that the Romanians could now help the Red Army defeat Hungary. In December 1944 the siege of Budapest began, with the Hungarian capital falling to the Red Army on February 13th.

What had once been Czechoslovakia was split up in 1939. Germany gained the western part of the country, Bohemia and Moravia. The Hungarians got much of the south of Slovakia and all of Ruthenia. The rump of Slovakia became a German satellite state.

With the invasion of the former Czechoslovakia, the Soviets were determined to get what they could for themselves. When Ruthenia was captured it was annexed by the USSR, and since 1991 it has been part of the Ukraine. This enabled the Soviets to have a direct route through to Prague, since all the territory north of Ruthenia, which had been Polish pre-1939, also became part of the USSR. The Red Army was to use this route among others to crush the 'Prague Spring' in 1968 and ensure Soviet rule.

The Bohemian part took some time to conquer, and in fact German resistance continued until after VE-Day, as described above. Some of the most fanatical of all SS forces fought the Red Army both in Hungary and in Bohemia, with the result that the casualties were enormous. Here too Hitler's zeal for defending absolutely everything to the last inch was against him. The last ever German offensive was a final desperate try in Hungary to stem the Soviet tide. This not only failed but also meant that those forces were not available for the defence of the central part of the Reich itself, Berlin included.

(Similarly hundreds of thousands of German troops ended

the war miles from their homeland, some in Courland, on the Baltic, and others in Norway, to defend that country against a British invasion that never came. In all, probably over a million German soldiers were scattered over Europe, surrendering only on VE-Day when the Reich itself was conquered.)

One of the controversial decisions at the end of the war was on whose army would liberate Prague. The Red Army's progress across Bohemia was slow, and from the West Patton's forces were racing towards the outer borders of that region at much greater speed. Patton would himself have loved to free Prague from the Germans, and in his case, to have achieved this consciously before the Red Army arrived.

But as with the race to Berlin, pre-existing military arrangements had to be kept, and Eisenhower forbade a disappointed Patton from sending some of his spare troops to liberate the Czechoslovak capital.

Since there was a Communist coup in Prague in 1948, that imposed Soviet rule on Czechoslovakia down until 1989, people have speculated whether or not the Americans rather than the Red Army liberating the city in 1945 would have made a difference. The Soviets, as throughout the Communist bloc of 1945–1989, always used the Red Army liberation of the region from the Nazis as psychological and moral justification for Communist rule. On that score, Patton arriving first in Prague might have made a subtle difference. However, as with all such things, it is interesting to contemplate, but ultimately impossible to tell.

Some 860,000 Germans surrendered to the Red Army in the conquest of southern Central Europe. Many wanted to flee to the West to surrender to British or American forces rather than to the

Soviets. The British took a dim view of this. As Montgomery so aptly remarked to Germans in that position, if they did not want to surrender to the Russians, they should not have invaded Russia in the first place!

But for most of this region, liberation from Nazi rule (or alliance, as in Hungary or Romania) meant over forty years of Soviet-imposed domination. For millions of Central Europeans, freedom from foreign rule did not end until 1989 and the fall of the Iron Curtain. For such peoples, 1945 was simply a change of despot. Only in Western Europe, thanks to the USA, did real freedom return.

PART SIX: II

1945

The Western Front and the End of the War in Europe

THE BRIDGE AT REMAGEN AND THE ROAD TO BERLIN

March 7th 1945

In March 1945 none of the Allied forces expected any of the bridges across the river Rhine to be intact. The presumption was that the Germans would have blown all of them, and so to find one that could still be used was a brilliant piece of good luck. American soldiers of the 9th Armoured Division, part of the First Army, were surprised to find and capture the Ludendorff Bridge at Remagen. This event on March 7th became one of the iconic moments of the war.

They had captured a railway bridge. Since other kinds of transport were necessary, the 12th Army Group, under the overall command of General Bradley, swung into operation to secure their happy fortune. Troops were stationed on the other side of the bridge, to prevent recapture by the Germans. Pontoon bridges were also set up so that vehicles could drive across in parallel to the railway line.

All this unexpected news meant that the person whom the Allied leadership planned to cross the Rhine first – Field Marshal Montgomery and the British – had been pre-empted. Monty was not the only Field Marshal to feel out of sorts, since Hitler proceeded to sack Field Marshal von Rundstedt for failure to stop the Americans from crossing the Rhine.

Then just to add to Montgomery's humiliation in not getting there first, armoured troops under his great rival, Patton, crossed the Rhine at Oppenheim, near the Swiss border.

This was all good news for the Allies, but Eisenhower had wanted the official crossing to be further up than either Remagen or Oppenheim. In the end, Montgomery's 21st Army Group was able to accomplish this, in Operation Plunder, on the day originally scheduled, March 23rd, at Wesel. This location enabled the Allies to enter the heartland of German industry, the Ruhr, and to be able to capture the north German plain. Churchill was present for Monty's now not quite so historic Rhineland crossing for the airborne section, Varsity. In a typical Churchillian gesture, the Prime Minister urinated into the river to show his contempt for his Nazi enemies.

Plunder had taken a *long* time to put together, to the fury of Patton and other Americans, who were irate that the British had taken such time to follow up the unexpected breakthroughs at Remagen and Oppenheim. Here even those who normally defend Montgomery feel that he was too fastidious, and could have delivered more quickly. But the British suffered very few casualties in their crossing, and with German defeat increasingly inevitable, it was just as well.

There now came to a head a major source of division between the British, who were thinking along political as well as military lines, and the Americans, who were essentially only interested in winning the war. Montgomery had always wanted a major thrust to Berlin. Now that his 21st Army were in Germany, he thought that a quick dash across the north of the country would deliver the capture of Berlin, the ultimate trophy. This was something that Churchill also strongly desired – not so much for prestige – as for the symbolism of the capital of Nazi Germany being the first to Berlin.

However, as we saw, at the Yalta Conference between Churchill, Stalin and the dying Roosevelt, the three major Allies had *already* carved up their future zones of occupation of Germany. Berlin would be an island, under the victorious powers, surrounded by what all agreed would be the Soviet zone.

To the Americans therefore, the main item was to beat the Germans, and preferably with as few Allied casualties as possible. (Remember too that they were still thinking in terms of the expected ground war against Japan. Soldiers killed or seriously injured in Germany would be unavailable for the Pacific.) Eisenhower, acting on his own authority, but with the subsequent full support of General George C. Marshall, told Stalin that the Americans would keep to their existing plans. This was the now infamous SCAF-252 signal, about which entire books have been written. Montgomery of course was furious. But Eisenhower was, with good cause, very worried lest the Red Army get to Denmark first. As it happened, this turned out to be an acute judgement, since Montgomery was able to rescue the Danes from a potential 'liberation' by the Soviets, for which Denmark gave him one of the highest decorations in their gift.

Two non-political factors also backed this up. First, it was Bradley's estimate that maybe as many as 100,000 US soldiers would die in a fight to the end in Berlin. That was far too high a potential casualty rate, and Eisenhower agreed with that way of thinking. (Here it matters not that Bradley subsequently felt that figure was too high – what matters is what he thought at the time.) Second, the Red Army was only forty miles from Berlin. So why take a militarily risky step for what would, in effect, be a wholly political outcome.

The Americans stuck to their strategy and Churchill, to his great dismay, was overruled.

However, new research suggests that Stalin was profoundly influenced by the accidental success of the Allies at Remagen on March 7th. Soviet specialists now think that this event made the key difference to Stalin in his decision to speed up the Red Army capture of Berlin. The Soviet dictator then told his two Marshals, Zhukov and Konev, that there was serious danger that the West would reach the German capital first. (This was of course untrue, as Stalin knew.) Marshal Konev therefore announced that it was vital that the Red Army capture Berlin ahead of the others, and, as we shall soon see, Stalin then ordered the attack to begin.

Other than reasons of prestige – which were very important to Stalin – historians have wondered why he was so keen not only to beat the West to Berlin but to be seen to do it as well.

Was it, as Antony Beevor has speculated, the wish of the NKVD to get to Dahlem, one of the suburbs, where the German atomic weapons research programme was being carried out? Would the idea of getting as much uranium as possible be motivation enough for Berlin?

Another Soviet specialist, Evan Mawdsley in *Thunder in the East*, suggests that Stalin had invested so much psychological effort and his own prestige into the capture of Berlin that he could not possibly let the West get there before him. In addition, the Red Army, which was in occupation of most of Central and Eastern Europe, wanted to have the kudos of conquering Hitler's lair, as part of their justification for the permanent Soviet control of so-called liberated territory. (Right down to 1989 large Soviet tanks from the war could be seen in Central European cities, to remind the people living there how grateful they should be for the Red Army rescuing them from fascism in 1944–1945.)

Stalin was also paranoid about Operation Sunrise, the attempt by the American OSS (the CIA's precursor) in Switzerland to obtain an early surrender from German troops in Italy. This would, of course, have been a breach of the unconditional surrender doctrine. Roosevelt was adamant, just before his own death, in telling Stalin that any thought of a separate Western peace with the Third Reich was nothing but a 'vile misrepresentation'. But Stalin, worried about the implications of Remagen, and about the talks in Switzerland (led by future CIA Director Allen Dulles), worried obsessively about the issue all the same. As he told a delegation of visitors to Moscow at the time:

'We are whipping the Germans and it's almost over. But keep in mind that the Allies will try to save the Germans and come to terms with them. We will be merciless with the Germans, but the Allies will try to settle things in a gentler way.'

This was all complete nonsense. Churchill and Montgomery might have been upset, but Eisenhower and Marshall were adamant, as was Truman to be when he became President on Roosevelt's death. No brave American – or Briton or Canadian – would die for Berlin. The Western Allies kept their word.

But Remagen had rattled Stalin badly. The attack on Berlin was speeded up by two weeks, and the competition he had set between his two Marshals, Zhukov and Konev, to get there first, now began. Remagen might have been a small bridge and a wonderful accident. But the success in capturing the Ludendorff Bridge across the River Rhine might well, if these historians are correct, have shortened the war.

PART SIX: III

1945

The War Against Japan and the End of the Fighting

THE BOMBING OF DRESDEN
AND TOKYO

February 13th–15th 1945 and March 9th–10th 1945

Allied raids on Dresden in February 1945 and Tokyo the following month are two of the most concentrated bombing raids on single city targets in history. The USAAF and principally the RAF were responsible for the Dresden bombings, while the Americans bombed Tokyo.

Yet while Dresden lives on in infamy, one of the most controversial decisions of the Western Allies in World War II, the firebombing of Tokyo less than a month later is often ignored. The reason for this could be because Tokyo was followed in August 1945 with the atom bomb blasts over Hiroshima and Nagasaki, which inaugurated a whole new scale of warfare and changed it permanently.

One hopes though that the ethnicity of the victims does not

play a part? As we have seen, both German and Japanese soldiers committed some of the worst barbarities in human history. But we do not, at least in the West, live in a world in which the innocent families or fellow citizens of such criminals have to suffer for the guilt of their kinsmen. The Holocaust or the extermination of twenty-seven million Soviet inhabitants does not justify wiping out tens of thousands of German civilians. Nor does the 'Rape of Nanking' exonerate those who obliterated similar numbers of Japanese.

An interesting recent study has suggested that to Germans, the Second World War means not just defeat but also the Holocaust. Germans have therefore repented of the sins of their recent ancestors and the country has now been a secure democracy for decades. However to the Japanese, the conflict means Hiroshima, an attack on a peaceful city that they regard as wholly innocent. Consequently the Japanese have never been seen to be as repentant as their German counterparts. Nationalism is acceptable in Japan even in the twenty-first century in a way it has long since stopped being in Germany.

Perhaps it is this contrast that also makes the difference to why the aura of Allied shame exists in relation to Dresden that it does not with the Tokyo fire raid. Considerably more people died in the latter than the former. It is guessed that about 40,000 or so people died in the Dresden raid, many of them, especially sadly, Allied prisoners of war. (One of this group, but who happily survived, was the America novelist Kurt Vonnegut, whose writing on that experience made the raid more famous still.) With Tokyo, the lowest death toll figures are about 88,000 people killed, although many would estimate the actual figure to be 124,000 or perhaps even higher still. If that is the case then at least three times more people died in Tokyo than in Dresden. Not only that, but far more died in Tokyo than in either of the atom bomb explosions taken individually. Conventional weapons ended more lives than the latest military technology.

By February 1945 the Soviets were on the edge of the final victory push to Berlin. The Allies were about to cross the River Rhine. The military or political justification for Dresden was thus slight, and the fact that it was in any case not a place of strategic value makes the raid even more inexcusable.

Churchill was now unhappy at the scale and nature of destruction, and so informed the Chiefs of Staff. But the Chief of Air Staff, Portal, strongly backed the decisions of 'Bomber Harris', who, to the end, insisted that such slaughter was militarily justifiable.

Altogether the Allied bombing of civilian targets in Germany led to at least 600,000 non-combatant deaths and the injuries of 800,000 or more, many of whom were women and children. This is far more than the number of civilians killed in Britain by the Luftwaffe, though of course it is a substantially lower figure than the ten million civilians slaughtered in the USSR in 1941–1945. With Japan, some 410,000 civilians were to die in the USAAF raids in 1945 alone. It seems that MacArthur was against such carnage, but that General Curtis Le May, in charge of the USAAF bombing policy, strongly backed raids on such targets.

All in all though, the raids on purely civilian areas, embodied by those on Dresden and Tokyo, are not the finest hour of the Western allies such as Britain and the USA. They were much debated at the time, and the perspective of history over the succeeding decades has not smiled upon them with approval.

THE BATTLE OF IWO JIMA

February 19th–March 25th 1945

Some battles become iconic because of what happened there. Others are now famous because of photography, a tool that became open to intrepid photographers from the mid-nineteenth century onwards. Iwo Jima, fought in early 1945 is such an encounter.

In and of itself the island is tiny – about two miles by four miles. Most historians agree that Iwo Jima had no real strategic significance since it was too small for an effective airbase from which to bomb both the Japanese fleet and mainland Japan itself. Instead its main use would be as an aircraft repair depot, especially for bombers that could still fly but which had suffered damage.

The death toll on Iwo Jima for the US Marine Corps would

prove exceedingly high for a bomber repair base. The Japanese were well dug in to the entire island, with all the natural advantages that this conveyed to the defenders. In addition, the forces under General Tadamichi Kuribayashi were unusually determined to fight to the end, as their commander was very familiar with the USA. He had briefly attended Harvard and more important had served as an attaché in the Japanese Embassy in Washington DC. This was a defender who knew his enemy.

The attack began on an unfortunate footing. The Marines had asked for a week of bombardment, but in the end the US Navy thought that three days were sufficient. With the Japanese so well defended, the American fire proved inadequate. The result was that the Marines found themselves under massive attack as soon as they got off the beach – their ease of landing had been deceptive.

Despite heavy losses the US Marine Corps were able, on February 23rd, to seize Mount Suribachi, the place from which much of the Japanese bombardment had come. It was the planting of the American flag, the Stars and Stripes, on the mountain's summit by a combination of five Marines and one hospital orderly that became famous.

But in fact the photograph, by war cameraman Joe Rosenthal, was the *second* time the flag was raised. Earlier on a dozen Marines had accomplished this feat of bravery, but the photograph of the *first* attempt took a long while to reach the USA. Rosenthal was with Associated Press, and his picture, of a smaller group of men, got back to America virtually immediately.

This photo, according to the editors of *US Camera Magazine*, 'recorded the soul of a nation'. Not surprisingly Rosenthal went on to win a Pulitzer Prize, for what has been justly called 'one of the most famous photographs in history'.

Other iconic photos taken in 1945 were also posed as we shall see. But although it was the second, not first, flag raising that we all know today, the feats of sheer bravery against hideous odds by the US Marines were as intrepid as the picture suggests.

The cost of Iwo Jima was colossal. Of the 20,000 Japanese troops on the island only 52 allowed themselves to be captured. Two of those who surrendered committed suicide. General Kuribayashi is presumed to have died fighting alongside his men. The US Marine casualties were 6,821 deaths and 19,217 injured, many seriously. It was a very high price. No fewer than twenty-seven Marines received the Medal of Honor of the US Congress, their highest decoration for bravery in combat (the equivalent of the British Victoria Cross).

The price of victory for the USA was getting ever greater.

THE BATTLE OF OKINAWA

April 1st–June 22nd 1945

The battle for the key island of Okinawa, the final staging post before Japan, was one of the most savage of the war in the Pacific. It was far larger than Iwo Jima – some eighty miles long and in some parts eighteen miles wide. This time the US Navy was determined to unleash as much firepower as possible, to avoid the Iwo Jima mistake. US Army Air Force bombers stuck mainly to attacks on the mainland, however, so the Navy bombarded the island for a whole week, with a naval invasion force of no less than 1,300 ships.

On April 1st, 50,000 Americans landed (200,000 by the end of the operation), against some 120,000 Japanese. The defenders decided as normal on waging a war of attrition against the invaders and it took nearly three months for the US forces to clear the island. One of their major problems was the Japanese *kamikaze* attacks, which were strange and alien for the Americans under fire. Furthermore, the *kamikazes* were not unsuccessful, damaging some 245 ships and sinking the US Carrier *Franklin*, with the loss of 725 crew on that ship alone. All in all the US Navy lost over 5,000 men, their biggest single loss since Pearl Harbor back in 1941.

The Japanese had constructed the world's largest battleship, the *Yamamoto*. But a naval era had come to an end, and it was expenditure wasted, since the ship was sunk; and 5,900 Japanese planes were sunk in return for 793 from the US Navy.

As always, figures are hard to judge, since estimates vary so wildly.

Some 7,600 US military (army and Marine Corps) were killed, with up to 75,000 casualties, including the injured, altogether. It is thought that ninety per cent or more of the 120,000 Japanese soldiers were killed. As for the civilian death toll, it is possible that as many as 150,000 Japanese died, a higher figure than the military deaths, and many of which were suicides of citizens who did not want to face dishonour in surrendering to the Americans.

Evan Mawdsley is among plenty of other historians when he comments that Okinawa was 'for the Americans the worst of any of the Pacific operations'.

For the USA the key question was this – if Okinawa was as bad as it was, what on earth would the invasion of the Japanese home island be like? The planned Allied assault on Kyushu was codenamed Olympic, and was scheduled for November. March 1946 would see Coronet, the invasion of Honshu.

The best estimate for Allied casualties – as the British were now expected to be able to join in as well with the liberation of Burma – were *270,000 deaths*. Remember that in the actual war, which we know finished in August, the *total* US death toll was around 300,000 deaths. So as many would die in the liberation of the Japanese main islands as in the whole of the rest of the war to that date. Other estimates made at the time had a far higher overall toll, with as many as a million casualties, injured as well as dead.

That is an astonishingly high figure. We now understand the effects of the atomic weapons that the US decided to employ, but we have to remember that back in July 1945 such bombs had been tested but were completely unknown in both their power and effects. And the prospect of war well into 1946, of American troops who had survived Europe having now to risk their lives to fight Japan, all concentrated the US government's minds.

As we shall now see . . .

THE FINAL DAYS OF THE WAR IN EUROPE

April 16th–May 8th 1945

The 'final days' of Adolf Hitler and of the war in Europe have been some of the most written about in history. Whole libraries could be filled with titles about the period April–May 1945. This is now so true that at least one book simply states that so much is known about this grand finale to the war that it need not be described in detail.

It is certainly the case that so much of it is exciting that to try to give details might be needless, as works such as those by Antony Beevor or Max Hastings have done it in a way that have enthralled millions.

A summary would be useful though. And there are probably many facets of the end of the European part of the Second World War which are not so well-known and therefore do need mention.

Soviet Marshal Zhukov finally unleashed the attack on Berlin on April 16th 1945. After all the delays, the endgame was now underway. But it was not that simple. Stalin had, in effect, become his own Eisenhower as well as being his own Truman, commander-in-chief in practice as well as in theory. Everything decided at the front had to be referred back to Moscow. And Stalin had decided to make the capture of Berlin a race between two very powerful rivals, Marshal Zhukov and Marshal Konev. Not a few Red Army soldiers would die in either friendly fire or in the sheer chaos of having two gigantic Soviet army groups both battling to reach the centre of Berlin first.

Zhukov in fact began slowly, more so than he would have liked. The Battle of the Seelow Heights, the capture of key outposts of the road to Berlin, took much longer than he would have wished, despite the sheer volume of firepower launched upon the increasingly hapless German defenders. Stalin was to goad Zhukov by comparing him unfavourably with Konev, and vice-versa.

The grotesque last days in the Berlin Bunker, with Hitler and his entourage increasingly living in the realms of total fantasy, is now famous. But in fact Hitler had only been in Berlin effectively since January 1945, having spent much of the war either at the Wolf's Lair in Prussia, or in his forward headquarters in the Ukraine, and those when not at his mountain retreat in Bavaria. What is interesting about Hitler's surreal time in the bunker is that he was there at all, since he had hardly spent any of the war in Berlin.

His final birthday party on April 20th must have been a bizarre occasion, with many of the guests thinking principally of flight, to escape before the Soviets came. He married his long-time mistress Eva Braun on April 29th, dictated his viscerally anti-Semitic last testament, and then committed suicide on April 30th.

It is easy to forget that the war continued for just over another week. Berlin itself fell on May 2nd. The iconic photo of Red Army soldiers raising the Soviet Red Flag over the Reichstag building was, like the similar picture of the US Marines in Iwo Jima, a staged shot. But despite that, it deserves to be famous, to celebrate the final capture of the enemy's capital city. Success had taken no fewer than 352,425 Soviet casualties, of which around a third were deaths.

Hitler, in his paranoia of betrayals at the end, had nominated Grand Admiral Dönitz to succeed him as Führer. By now there was no hope of success for the Third Reich, and the attempts of Himmler to negotiate a peace via Sweden failed utterly. No one would negotiate with the Nazis, however paranoid Stalin might have felt in suspecting his Western colleagues.

But because of Soviet suspicions, VE-Day had to happen twice. The first surrender was to the West, to Eisenhower in Rheims, and to Montgomery in northern Germany on Luneburg Heath. Then it happened all over again, to the Soviets in Berlin.

Either way though, on May 8th 1945 the war in Europe was over. What is frightening to contemplate is the death toll for just those last five months, January to May 1945. During that time, when the collapse of Nazism had long since been inevitable, some 1.4 million German soldiers died, fighting to save an already doomed regime. And because of the way in which Stalin chose to conclude the fighting on the Eastern Front, no fewer than 770,000 Red Army soldiers died during the same five-month period. That means that from January to May 1945 more than twice as many Soviet forces died than all the British and American casualties for the entire war put together.

Red Army soldiers raped some one million German women, with over 10,000 dying as a result. Western soldiers were not perfect, but the way in which Soviet forces ended the war delegitimised the whole Communist system from the beginning. The behaviour of the Red Army was never forgotten in all the forty-four years of Soviet rule over Central Europe, a shadow that was cast permanently throughout the Cold War. Not for several months did the Soviet leadership realise the long-term effects that such pillage would have on areas of Europe that they now sought to occupy and establish Communist rule.

But for millions of people, VE-Day brought freedom, liberation and an end to war. If you lived in Western Europe, the years of strife were truly over.

HIROSHIMA AND NAGASAKI

August 6th and 9th 1945

Anyone who visits the Truman Presidential Library in Independence, Missouri will see a plaque asking visitors to discuss and ponder the morality of the two atomic bombs dropped on Japan in August 1945.

The decision to use such extraordinary weapons of mass destruction has been debated hotly ever since. Tens of thousands of people died in each blast, the overwhelming majority of them innocent civilians.

It is also zealously contested because it is unclear whether or not Japan would have surrendered anyway. The Japanese government had originally put out peace feelers via the Soviet government, with whom as we saw they had signed a crucial neutrality pact back in April 1941. But Stalin had also promised the Western Allies that he was going to break that agreement once VE-Day was over, and he was to keep that promise. Red Army units duly invaded northern China and attacked the Japanese forces there with much vigour.

Writers such as Max Hastings (in his case in several of his works) have suggested that morally the decision to drop the bombs was the right one, as it really did shorten the war. There were those fanatics in Japan who were determined come what may to resist to the bitter end, whatever the Emperor might decree. A coup came within an inch of taking place. It would have continued Japanese fighting, and therefore a hideous greater civilian death toll even without a third atom bomb.

By August 1945 the Allies were exhausted with war. The USSR had lost tens of millions, and while British and American casualties were infinitely lower, both of those nations were also weary of the toll they had been obliged to pay because of the aggression of others. The Japanese use of *kamikaze* pilots, something so alien and fanatical in Western eyes, had hardened many in the USA against Japan. An atom bomb might be a drastic way of giving vent to one's feelings about the nature of the Japanese enemy, but given the context of the time it is perhaps an understandable decision.

The US government, now under the new and inexperienced President Harry Truman, had the ability to read all the supposedly top secret Japanese diplomatic codes, so knew precisely what the Imperial government was thinking.

And despite Roosevelt's insistence on unconditional surrender, it is interesting that the Allies did agree that the position of Emperor should be maintained, albeit as a cipher head of state stripped of divine status. Truman, more than aware of the vast US death toll in the capture of Okinawa, felt that a ground invasion of Japan would lead to 'an Okinawa from one end of Japan to another . . .' The US terror was hundreds of thousands of American casualties. As President of the USA it was only natural that Truman should think of the Allied death toll over and above the number of Japanese who might die.

When the *Enola Gay* dropped the first bomb on Hiroshima on August 6th 1945, some 80,000 people were incinerated, and a further 35,000 were injured. It is hard to calculate how many people died long term from the effects of the blast.

Stalin's declaration of war on Japan on August 8th ended Japanese hopes that the USSR could act as an intermediary. Some Japanese, astonishingly, wanted to continue even after both Hiroshima and the invasion of Imperial forces in China. So the 'Fat Man' was dropped on Nagasaki on August 9th. This time only 40,000 died. It was a strange choice for the USA, since Nagasaki is also one of the few cities in Japan with a large Christian population.

Still the Japanese did not surrender – the War Council was three to three, and thus deadlocked. But one of those voting for surrender was the Emperor, and as the Americans agreed he could continue, this eventually made the critical difference.

Fighting on the Chinese mainland continued until August 21st, but there were still Japanese forces that needed to surrender and be disarmed, and that continued until October 24th, long after the formal cessation of war. VJ-Day was September 2nd, on board the USS *Missouri*, moored in Tokyo Bay. The Japanese formally surrendered to the Allies.

World War II was over at last.

CONCLUSION: WHO WON?

Eight years (1937–1945) and eighty million deaths later, who won the Second World War?

It is an important question since the answer is not as obvious as it seems. Britain, for example, was on the winning side. But the UK was broke, and many years of hardship followed. Even rationing was not finally abolished until into the 1950s. The British Empire, the source of so much pride both to Churchill and to millions of others, soon morphed into a Commonwealth, with India, the 'Jewel in the Crown', gaining independence in 1947 and as two countries not one. By the 1960s most of the colonies were independent nations.

At least the bloodshed in losing its Empire was not as considerable for the British – exceptions such as Kenya notwithstanding – as it was for France. The French were given back their imperial possessions in South East Asia only to lose them in the humiliation and defeat of Dien Ben Phu in 1954, in Vietnam. The violent loss of Algeria followed not long later.

Britain and France, therefore, were winners and losers at the same time, still powerful nations (both today in the G8) but not what they had been before.

The USA was unquestionably a winner though in every possible sense. America was far more prosperous after the war than it had been before. The need for mammoth-scale military production created not just jobs but long-term prosperity with it. The US became in reality what it had been in disguise before 1939, the world's leader and democratic superpower. However mighty Britain might have thought itself even as late as the 1930s, there was no question by 1945 that the baton had been passed to its former American colony. Now the US was a nation with more resources and power than the British had ever possessed.

How about the USSR though – was it a winner in the long run as well as in 1945? From 1945–1991 the Soviet Union had every appearance of being a superpower. The USSR certainly felt itself to be one, the rival to the USA for status and dominance in what political scientists call the *bipolar* world (using that word in the geopolitical sense).

New thinking however suggests that the need to maintain so vast an empire, and to play endless military catch-up with the USA, eventually bankrupted a nation and system that was inherently unable to sustain such a role. Victory in 1945, along with the death in 1941–1945 of no fewer than twenty-seven million of its citizens, disguised the inevitability of long-term decline.

Russia in the twenty-first century could be described in the same way as Dean Acheson, the American Secretary of State, once described Britain: a once great superpower that had lost an Empire and not yet found a role. The story of Russia since 1991, with the strong nostalgia for glory days now long gone by, is similar to the feelings of many English people at the similar loss of superpower status by 1945. Russia and Britain won against Hitler, but in the current century are not the major players that they had been decades and centuries earlier.

Many would argue that in a strange way Germany and Japan were both losers in 1945 and winners ever since. Japan is a difficult country to assess, since its once unstoppable economic miracle came to an end, and in the current century it is uncertain where that nation wishes to go. Germany however, after its much more lasting and effective economic wonder years, has gone on to be the leader of Western Europe, the number one player increasingly politically as well as financially. It is also now a vibrant and genuine democracy, a nation now at peace with itself, especially as, unlike Japan, it has properly renounced and repented of past misdeeds.

China in 1945 was a winner, but also a major basket case, with a violent civil war that went on to kill millions more people on top of the twenty million or so lost in 1937–1945. The inability of the Nationalist government to defeat Japan so weakened the corrupt regime that Mao's Communist takeover in 1949 was surely inevitable. As we now know, tens of millions – maybe as many as forty million or more – would die in man-created famines under Mao, as the new government sought to impose its ideology on the people.

Now however many argue that China will be the superpower of the twenty-first century. Historically, looked at over millennia and not just centuries, the Chinese Empire was always more powerful in a global sense than the mighty but still comparatively small empires of Europe or Latin America. It could be, as some suggest, that Chinese dominance is the norm, and that the recent centuries of European and European-descended American hegemony is a blip.

But these are controversial and still-hotly debated issues. Just as a history of the world written post-1945 but pre-1989 would now seem strange because it did not see the end of the Cold War, predictions far into the twenty-first century could be equally flawed. (After all, who would have predicted 9/11 before 2001 and its results?)

One thing is for certain, though. Now well over six decades since the end of the war in 1945 we have not experienced carnage and global war on that scale since then. Internal bloodbaths such as in Maoist China and comparatively smaller conflicts post-1991 have taken place. But we can be profoundly thankful that a war across continents and with eighty million dead has not happened again. World War III might have been predicted, but never took place. The world now knows the price of such conflict, and has not repeated the mistake.

KEY COMMANDERS OF WORLD WAR II

Note: British titles can be confusing, so I have named British Commanders as they were known during the war, rather than with their post-war titles. I have also put *Soviet* instead of *Russian* as not all USSR officers were ethnic Russians

Alexander, Field Marshal Sir Harold, 1891–1969 (*British*) Churchill's favourite general; notionally Montgomery's superior in 1942 and Supreme Allied Commander in Italy and then the Mediterranean 1944–1945.

Antonov, Alexei, 1896–1962 (*Soviet*) Soviet Chief of the General Staff in 1944–1945.

Arnold, HH 'Hap', 1886–1950 (*American*) Commanding

General of the US Army Air Force from 1942.

Auchinleck, Field Marshal Sir Claude, 1884–1981 (*British*) Commander-in-Chief Middle East 1941–1942 and then in India.

Badoglio, Marshal Pietro, 1871–1936 (*Italian*) Italian commander who opposed Italian entry into war in 1940 and who overthrew Mussolini in 1943.

Bock, Field Marshal Fedor von, 1880–1945 (*German*) Commander of Operation Typhoon in 1941 and of Army Group South in 1942.

Bradley, General of the Army Omar, 1893–1981 (*American*) Commander of the 12th Army Group 1944–1945, effectively of US troops in NW Europe.

Brooke, Field Marshal Sir Alan, 1883–1963 (*British*) Chief of the Imperial General Staff 1941–1946.

Chiang Kai-shek, 1887–1975 (in Pinyin Jiang Jieshi; *Chinese*) Political and military leader of the Nationalist-controlled part of China during the war.

Churchill, Sir Winston, 1874–1965 (*British*) Prime Minister and Minister of Defence 1940–1945. He rescued his country in 1940.

Clark, Mark, 1896–1945 (*American*) American commander in Italy 1943–1945 and of 15th Army Group there 1944–1945.

Crerar, Henry, 1888–1965 (*Canadian*) Commanded Canadian troops in NW Europe 1944–1945.

Cunningham, Admiral of the Fleet Sir Alan, 1883–1963 (*British*) First Sea Lord 1943–1945 and victor of naval battles against the Italians in 1940–1941.

De Gaulle, General Charles, 1890–1940 (*French*) Leader of the Free French in exile 1940–1944 and thereafter a leader of France and President 1958–1969.

Dill, Field Marshal Sir John, 1881–1944 (*British*) Chief of the Imperial General Staff 1940–1941 and Head of the British Joint Staff Mission to the USA 1941–1944; the only non-American buried at Arlington National Cemetery.

Dönitz, Grand Admiral Karl, 1891–1980 (*German*) Dönitz was in charge of U-Boats and then Commander-in-Chief of the German Navy 1943–1945 and briefly President of Germany in succession to Hitler in 1945.

Dowding, Air Chief Marshal Sir Hugh, 1882–1970 (*British*) Commander-in-Chief of Bomber Command during the Battle of Britain in 1940.

Eisenhower, General Dwight, 1890–1969 (*American*) American commander above all as Supreme Allied Commander in NW Europe 1944–1945; President of the USA 1953–1961.

Freyberg, General Sir Bernard, 1889–1963 (*New Zealander*) Commander of the New Zealand forces in North Africa and Europe 1940–1945 and the commander during the fall of Crete in 1941.

Gavin, James, 1907–1990 (*American*) Commander of the 82nd Airborne Division in 1944–1945, including for Market Garden.

Göring, Hermann, 1893–1946 (*German*) Former First World War fighter ace who was an early Nazi Party recruit and was in charge of the Luftwaffe during the war.

Gort, Field Marshal Viscount, 1886–1946 (*British*) Chief of the Imperial General Staff 1937–1939 and commander of the BEF in France 1939–1940.

Guderian, Heinz, 1888–1954 (*German*) Successful German Panzer commander in France and on the Eastern Front but who quarrelled with Hitler.

Halder, Franz, 1884–1972 (*German*) Chief of Staff at OKH (German military headquarters) from 1938–1942.

Halsey, Admiral William, 1882–1959 (*American*) Commander of the US Third Fleet in the Pacific against Japan.

Harris, Marshal of the RAF Sir Arthur known as Bomber Harris, 1892–1984 (*Rhodesian*) Controversial Air Officer Commanding-in-Chief of RAF Bomber Command 1942–1945.

Hitler, Adolf, 1889–1945 (*German*) German leader 1933–1945.

Hodges, Courtney, 1887–1966 (*American*) Commanded the US First Army 1944–1945 in NW Europe.

Horrocks, General Sir Brian, 1895–1985 (*British*) One of Montgomery's key subordinates during the war including XXX Corps during Market Garden.

Horton, Admiral Sir Max, 1883–1951 (*British*) Commanded the British effort in the war against U-Boats in the Atlantic during much of the war.

Hoth, Herman, 1885–1971 (*German*) A key German General on the Eastern Front and leading Panzer commander until dismissed in 1943.

Ismay, General Sir Lionel 'Pug', 1887–1965 (*British*) Churchill's personal Chief of Staff 1940–1945.

Keitel, Field Marshal Wilhelm, 1882–1946 (*German*) Chief of the High Command of the Armed Forces 1938–1946.

Kesselring, Field Marshal Albert, 1885–1960 (*German*) Chief of Staff of the Luftwaffe before the war and a German commander during it, mainly during the war in Italy 1943–1945 and Commander-in-Chief West during 1945.

King, Admiral Ernest, 1878–1956 (*American*) Commander-in-Chief of the US Fleet 1941–1945 and Chief of Naval Operations 1942–1945.

Kinkaid, Admiral Thomas, 1888–1972 (*American*) Commanded the Seventh Fleet 1943–1945.

Kleist, Field Marshal Paul von, 1881–1854 (*German*) Panzer general and commander of Army Group A on the Eastern Front 1942–1944.

Kluge, Field Marshal Hans von, 1882–1944 (*German*) Commander on the Eastern Front and then Commander-in-Chief West until committing suicide in 1944 because of suspected links to the July Bomb Plot conspirators.

Konev, Marshal Ivan, 1897–1973 (*Soviet*) One of the top Soviet commanders on the Eastern Front and in charge of the First Ukrainian Front in 1945 in the capture of Berlin.

Leahy, Admiral William, 1875–1959 (*American*)

Roosevelt's personal Chief of Staff 1941–1945.

Leclerc, Jacques, (wartime pseudonym) 1902–1947 (*French*) Free French general during the war whose troops liberated Paris in 1944.

Lee-Mallory, Air Chief Marshal Sir Trafford, 1892–1944 (*British*) Commander of 12 Group Fighter Command during the Battle of Britain.

LeMay, General Curtis, 1906–1990 (*American*) Commanded the XXI Bomber command in the destruction of Japan during the last part of the war.

List, Field Marshal Siegmund, 1880–1971 (*German*) Commanded German armies in Poland, France and the Balkans and of the failed conquest of the Caucasus in 1942.

MacArthur, General of the Army Douglas, 1880–1964 (*American*) Former Army Chief of Staff who commanded the successful series of battles in the Pacific as Supreme Allied Commander SW Pacific 1942–1945.

McAuliffe, General Anthony, 1898–1975 (*American*) Commander of US forces in Bastogne during the Battle of the Bulge: it was he who told the Germans 'Nuts' rather than surrender to them.

Manstein, Field Marshal Fritz Erich von, 1887–1983

(*German*) Commander behind the successful Ardennes campaign against France in 1940 and of Army Group South on the Eastern Front 1943–1944.

Marshall, General George, 1880–1959 (*American*) Chief of Army Staff 1939–1945, the outstanding American who Churchill described as the 'organiser of victory' and after the war famous for his Marshall Plan to rescue Europe from starvation and economic collapse.

Model, Field Marshal Walter, 1891–1945 (*German*) Commanded on the Eastern Front and then Army Group B in NW Europe 1944–1945.

Montgomery, Field Marshal Sir Bernard, 1888–1976 (*British*) Britain's most prominent and controversial commander, including of the 8th Army at Alamein in 1942 and of 21st Army Group in NW Europe 1944–1945; his career is one that has been continually debated since the war itself.

Mountbatten, Admiral Lord Louis, 1900–1979 (*British*) Chief of Combined Operations 1942–1943 and Supreme Allied Commander South East Asia 1943–1945 and later Viceroy of India and Chief of the Defence Staff.

Mussolini, Benito, 1883–1945 (*Italian*) Dictator (*Duce* or leader) of Italy 1922–1943 and then of a puppet government in northern Italy until 1945.

Nagumo, Chuichi, 1887–1944 (*Japanese*) Japanese admiral who lost at Midway.

Nimitz, Fleet Admiral Chester, 1885–1966 (*American*) Commander of the US Navy in the struggle against Japan 1941–1945 and now regarded as one of the greatest commanders of World War II.

O'Connor, General Sir Richard, 1889–1981 (*British*) The outstanding and successful commander of the Western Desert Force 1940–1941, who was tragically captured by the Germans.

Oikawa, Yasuji, 1883–1958 (*Japanese*) Chief of the Naval Staff in Japan 1944–1945.

Ozawa, Jisaburo, 1886–1966 (*Japanese*) Commander of the Third Fleet 1942–1944 (including at Leyte) and of the Combined Fleet in 1945.

Park, Air Chief Marshal Sir Keith, 1892–1975 (*New Zealander*) Heroic commander of 11 Group during the Battle of Britain then sidelined like Dowding.

Patch, General Alexander, 1889–1945 (*American*) Commanded both at Guadalcanal and the Seventh Army in Europe.

Patton, General George, 1885–1945 (*American*) One of

the best and most controversial US commanders of the war against Germany triumphing in charge of the Third Army 1944–1945.

Paulus, Field Marshal Friedrich, 1890–1957 (*German*) Unsuccessful commander of the Sixth Army in Stalingrad 1942–1943.

Perceval, General Sir Arthur, 1887–1966 (*British*) Unsuccessful commander of Singapore in 1942, who surrendered to the Japanese.

Portal, Marshal of the Royal Air Force Sir Charles, 1893–1971 (*British*) Chief of the Air Staff 1940–1945 and the service chief most esteemed by the USA.

Pound, Admiral of the Fleet Sir Dudley, 1877–1943 (*British*) First Sea Lord and Chief of Naval Staff 1939–1943.

Raeder, Grand Admiral Erich, 1876–1960 (*German*) Commander-in-Chief of the German Navy 1935–1943.

Ramsay, Admiral Sir Bertram, 1883–1945 (*British*) Naval commander in charge of the evacuation of the BEF in 1940 and who organised the naval side of D-Day in 1944.

Rokossovsky, Marshal Konstantin, 1896–1968 (*Soviet*) Successful Soviet commander on the Eastern Front, including Stalingrad and Kursk, and of the Second Belarus Front against Berlin.

Rommel, Field Marshal Erwin, 1891–1944 (*German*) The 'Desert Fox' in North Africa against the Allies 1941–1943 then in charge of Army Group B in France in 1944.

Roosevelt, Franklin, 1882–1945 (*American*) The great US President 1933–1945 in charge of the US war effort 1941–1945.

Rundstedt, Field Marshal Karl von, 1875–1953 (*German*) Key German commander throughout the war, on the Eastern and Western fronts, from the capture of Kiev in 1941 to the Battle of the Bulge in 1944.

Slim, Field Marshal Sir William, 1891–1970 (*British*) Most historians now rate him the best British commander of World War II; commanded the Fourteenth Army in Burma 1943–1945.

Spaatz, General Carl, 1891–1974 (*American*) Commanding General US Strategic Air Forces in Europe 1944–1945 and then a similar post in the Pacific.

Spruance, Admiral Raymond, 1886–1969 (*American*) Commanded the Fifth Fleet in the Pacific 1943–1945.

Stalin, Marshal Joseph, 1879–1953 (*Soviet*) Soviet

dictator throughout World War II, in neutrality with Hitler 1939–41 and with the Allies 1941–1945 and a man responsible for the death of millions during his rule.

Stauffenberg, Count Claus von, 1907–1944 (*German*) Organiser of the unsuccessful attempt to assassinate Hitler in 1944.

Stillwell, Joseph 'Vinegar Joe', 1883–1946 (*American*) In charge of American links with Nationalist China through much of the war.

Student, Colonel General Kurt, 1890–1978 (*German*) Parachute commander who led the invasion of Crete in 1941.

Sugiyama, Field Marshal Hajime, 1880–1945 (*Japanese*) One of the senior Japanese commanders throughout the war including Chief of the General Staff.

Taylor, General Maxwell, 1901–1987 (*American*) Commanded the US 101st Airborne Division.

Tedder, Marshal of the Royal Air Force Sir Arthur, 1890–1967 (*British*) Air Commander-in-Chief Mediterranean 1943 and Eisenhower's Deputy Supreme Allied Commander 1943–1945.

Terauchi, Field Marshal Hisaichi, 1879–1946 (*Japanese*) Commander-in-Chief of Japanese forces in SE Asia 1941–1945.

Tojo, General Hideki, 1884–1948 (*Japanese*) Prime Minister of Japan 1941–1944 and War Minister 1940–1941.

Wavell, Field Marshal Sir Archibald, 1883–1950 (*British*) Commander-in-Chief Middle East 1939–1941 and then in India where he went on to become Viceroy 1943–1947.

Wedemeyer, General Albert, 1897–1989 (*American*) Key staff officer early in the war and then commander of US forces in the China area.

Weygand, General Maxime, 1867–1965 (*French*) French commander in 1940 who later collaborated with Vichy.

Wilson, Field Marshal Sir Henry 'Jumbo', 1881–1964 (*British*) Served in the Middle East during the war and ended as Supreme Allied Commander Mediterranean 1944–1945.

Wingate, Brigadier Orde, 1903–1944 (*British*) Eccentric officer who invented the 'Chindit' guerrilla force to fight the Japanese in the jungle.

Yamamoto, Admiral Isoroku, 1884–1943 (*Japanese*)

Commander-in-Chief of the Combined Fleet in the Pacific 1939–1943.

Yamashita, General Tomoyuki, 1885–1946 (*Japanese*) The conqueror of Singapore in 1942 and in Manchuria and then the Philippines.

Zhukov, Marshal Georgi, 1896–1974 (*Soviet*) Now considered by many historians to be the best of the Allied commanders in the war; he held several posts 1941–1945 and masterminded the capture of Berlin in 1945.

SELECTED BIBLIOGRAPHY

Thousands of books have been written about World War II. Thankfully in recent years some excellent single-volume books have appeared, of which a selection appears below. I have selected more recent books where possible otherwise this list would be impossibly long. My other book on the war is an overview rather than the detailed battle guide that you are reading, so complements our book.

Alanbrooke, Field Marshal Lord, *War Diaries 1939–1945* (London, 2001)

Bard, Mitchell, *The Complete Idiots Guide to World War II* (New York, 2010)

Beevor, Antony, *The Second World War* (London, 2012)

Binns, Stuart and Wood, Adrian (ed.), *The Second World War in Colour* (London, 1999)

Burleigh, Michael, *Moral Combat* (London, 2011)

Catherwood, Christopher, *World War Two: A Beginner's Guide* (London, 2014)

Collingham, Lizzie, *The Taste of War: World War Two and the Battle for Food* (London, 2011)

Corrigan, Gordon, *The Second World War: A Military History* (London, 2010)

Farmelo, Graham, *Churchill's Bomb: A Hidden History of Science, War and Politics* (London, 2013)

Gilbert, Martin, *The Atlas of the Second World War* (London, 2008)

Hastings, Max, *All Hell Let Loose* (London, 2011)

Keegan, John, *The Battle for History* (London, 1995)

Kennedy, David, *The Library of Congress World War II Companion* (New York, 2007)

Kennedy, Paul, *Engineers of Victory* (London, 2013)

Mawdsley, Evan, *World War II: A New History* (Cambridge, 2009)

Overy, Richard, *Why the Allies Won* (London, 1995)

Roberts, Andrew, *The Storm of War* (London, 2009)

Stone, Norman, *World War Two: A Short History* (London, 2012)

Weinberg, Gerhard, *A World at Arms* (Cambridge, 1994)

NEW THOUGHTS ON THE EASTERN FRONT

Some fascinating, if controversial, new thinking has appeared in the past few years that puts the Eastern Front into its proper context. Those by Laurence Rees have also been compelling television documentaries of the same name.

Bellamy, Chris, *Absolute War* (London, 2007)

Davies, Norman, *Europe at War 1939–1945* (London, 2006)

Overy, Richard, *Russia's War* (London, 1997)

Rees, Laurence, The *War of the Century* (London, 1999)

— —. *World War Two: Behind Closed Doors* (London, 2008)

Roberts, Geoffrey, *Stalin's Wars* (London, 2006)

Snyder, Timothy, *Bloodlands: Europe Between Hitler and Stalin* (New York, 2010)

SUBJECT SPECIFIC TITLES
With preference for the more recent books

THE ORIGINS OF WAR

Brendon, Piers, *The Dark Valley* (London, 2000)

Carley, Michael Jabara, *1939: The Alliance That Never Was and the Coming of World War II* (Chicago, 1999)

Overy, Richard and Wheatcroft, Andrew, *The Road to War* (London, 2009)

Reynolds, David, *From Munich to Pearl Harbor* (Chicago, 2001)

Steiner, Zara, *The Triumph of the Dark* (Oxford, 2011)

SINO-JAPANESE WAR UP TO 1937–1941

Colvin, John, *Nomonhan* (London, 1999)

Ienaga, Saburo, *Japan's Last War: World War II and the Japanese, 1931–1945* (Oxford, 1979)

Mitter, Rana, *China's War with Japan 1937–1945* (London, 2013)

THE KEY BATTLES IN 1940 AND 1941

Horne, Alistair, *To Lose a Battle: France 1940* (London, 1969)

Kershaw, Ian, *Fateful Choices* (London, 2007)

Mawdsley, Evan, *December 1941* (London, 2011)

May, Ernest, *Strange Victory: Hitler's Conquest of France* (London, 2000)

THE EASTERN FRONT 1941–1943

Beevor, Antony, *Stalingrad* (London, 1998)

Braithwaite, Rodric, *Moscow 1941: A City and its People at War* (London, 2006)

Burleigh, Michael, *Germany Turns Eastwards: a study of Ostforschung in the Third Reich* (London, 2002)

Gorodetsky, Gabriel, *Grand Delusion: Stalin and the German Invasion of Russia* (New Haven, 1999)

Kershaw, Ian, *Hitler, The Germans and the Final Solution* (London, 2008)

Nagorski, Andrew, *The Greatest Battle: The Fight for Moscow 1941–1942* (London, 2007)

Mosier, John, *Deathride: Hitler vs. Stalin* (New York, 2010)

Stahel, David, *Operation Barbarossa and Hitler's Defeat in the East* (Cambridge, 2009)

— —. *Kiev 1941* (Cambridge, 2011)

— —. *Operation Typhoon* (Cambridge, 2013)

THE ASIAN AND PACIFIC WAR 1941–1944

Ambrose, Hugh, *The Pacific: Hell Was an Ocean Away* (Edinburgh, 2010)

Morison, Samuel Eliot, *The Two-Ocean War* (Boston, 1963)

THE AMERICANS AND BRITISH IN AFRICA AND EUROPE 1942–1944

Dimbleby, Jonathan, *Destiny in the Desert* (London, 2012)

Holland, James, *Together We Stand* (London, 2005)

— —. James *Dam Busters: The Race to Smash the Dams, 1943* (London, 2012)

THE ROAD TO BERLIN: EASTERN FRONT 1944–1945

Beevor, Antony, *Berlin: The Downfall 1945* (London, 2002)

Davies, Norman, *Rising '44: The Battle for Warsaw* (London, 2003)

THE END OF THE WAR IN WESTERN EUROPE
1944–1945

Beevor, Antony, *D-Day: The Battle for Normandy* (London, 2009)

Bennett, Gill, (ed.) *The End of the War in Europe, 1945: Conference Proceedings* (London, 1996)

Kershaw, Ian, *The End: Hitler's Germany 1944–1945* (London, 2011)

Hastings, Max, *Overlord* (London, 1984)

—— ——. *Armageddon: The Battle for Germany 1944–5* (London, 2004)

Holland, James, *Italy's Sorrow* (London, 2008)

THE END OF THE WAR AGAINST JAPAN 1944–1945

Hastings, Max, *Nemesis: The Battle for Japan 1944–1945* (London, 2007)

ACKNOWLEDGEMENTS

Most authors end their acknowledgements with a paean of thanks to their patient spouse. I think that it is better to start there rather than to finish, especially since my wife Paulette is the person without whom any of my books would ever get written. She is my constant muse and encouragement and my debt to her is always the deepest and the most profound.

This book began life in a Cambridge café. It started as a conversation with the legendary Heffer's bookseller, Richard Reynolds, and Susie Dunlop, publishing director at Allison & Busby.

Sadly my usual mentor for works such as this, Richard Holmes (the military rather than the literary writer of that name), is no longer with us. What a wonderful encouragement he was to so many fellow historians, all much less well known than he was but whom he did so much to help and to enthuse.

This book has been made possible by a three-year personal grant from the Royal Literary Fund, to whose generosity I am more than grateful. Eileen Gunn has been a pillar of support and helpfulness, and in conjunction with the Fund I am also very grateful to Hugh Bicheno, Nathan Buttery, Alasdair Paine and Andrew Whittaker in helping to make the grant possible.

My mother Elizabeth Catherwood, a survivor of the Blitz, has also been magnificently kind and supportive. She was at Oxford after the war with many of the servicemen who survived, one of whom, Geoffrey Drinkwater, is one of the dedicatees of this book, along with her brother-in-law Alan Clough. Geoffrey survived the Arctic Convoys and it is wonderful that the bravery of those who served with him has been recognised at last, even though it took nearly seventy years for their medals to be granted.

Much of the research for this has taken place in the fabulous surroundings of the Churchill Archives Centre at Churchill College Cambridge. Winston Churchill played a unique role during the Second World War. To be able to write surrounded by the archives of such a man, and in the library of leading naval historian Stephen Roskill, which is situated in the Centre, is a rare privilege. Allen Packwood and his team have been the embodiment of enthusiasm and helpfulness to countless historians over many years and I am most grateful to them both individually and corporately: Natalie Adams, Andrew Riley, Sophie Bridges, Katharine Thomson, Sarah Lewery, Julie Sanderson, Emily Morris, Louise Watling, Gemma Cook, and Liz Yamada.

My two Cambridge colleges, Churchill and St Edmund's, are great places in which to be based and I thank the Master and Fellows of both of them. Graham Farmelo has always been a wonderful source of encouragement, and his presence at Churchill has been a boon.

My writing is subsidised by my teaching for the Cambridge branch of the INSTEP programme. This brings the best and brightest students from select American universities (such as Tulane, Wake Forest, Villanova and sometimes others) to spend a term in Cambridge. Teaching keeps the mind alert and the fact that the students are a delight to be with makes the task all the better. The programme directors, Geoffrey Williams (the distinguished defence expert) and his wife Janice are a joy to work with and I am as thankful to them for making this book possible as I am for many others.

As always I am indebted to Andrew and Clare Whittaker, Alasdair and Rachel Paine, Nathan and Debbie Buttery, Jonquil Drinkwater and Andrew Kearsley, Richard and Sally Reynolds, the Marshall family of Virginia in the USA and supportive friends of my wife such as Betsy Weaver Brandt and Gill Smith, for years of friendship and encouraging my morale as well as Paulette's.

My legendary agent Andrew Hayward was not directly involved in the commissioning of this particular book but his advice and kindness has always been indispensable.

CHRISTOPHER CATHERWOOD

CAMBRIDGE, 2014